# Animal
## Line Drawing

Published in the United States by The Pigeon Letters, LLC.
www.thepigeonletters.com

Animal Line Drawing: Learn 150+ Step-by-Step Animals, Insects, Birds, Fish, and Other Cuties
ISBN 978-0-9985585-4-7

Design by Peggy Dean

10 9 8 7 6 5 4 3 2 1

First Edition

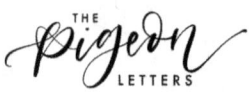

# Animal Line Drawing

Peggy Dean

DEDICATED TO MY DARLING KITTY CAT,
## LITTLE EDIE

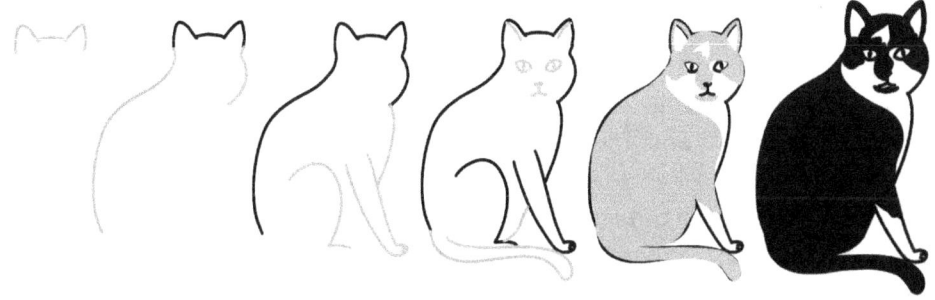

LUCKY FOR YOU, YOU GET TO DRAW HER
FIRST. YOU'RE WELCOME.

This simple line drawing guide features all of our favorite animals, insects, fish, birds, even dinosaurs and kitties! If you've journeyed through my first line drawing books, Botanical Line Drawing and BLD Cactus & Succulent Edition, you're probably familiar with the fun art of line drawing. If this is your first time, get ready for some fun!

Line drawing is a playful, sometimes delicate, and easier-then-you-probably-expect art form that doesn't require many materials, but still allows you to branch out and create something gorgeous by applying other types of art to your illustrations. Line drawings look lovely as standalone pieces, but also work well when incorporating other art media and styles.

This step-by-step book guides you through pages and pages of simple illustrated instructions, introducing 5 steps per illustration. You will see that each step adds onto the previous shape or line, and in no time, you'll have produced your very own coveted line drawings!

I encourage you to pull out a sketchbook and practice these animals separately, then bring them together to showcase animal habitats! Options are limitless with this art form.

Did you know there are more than 8 million species of animals in the world? While I wish I could have put every single one of them in this book, for now we'll enjoy this small curated collection. The world is incredible!

# contents

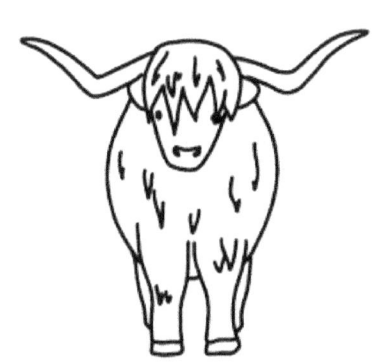

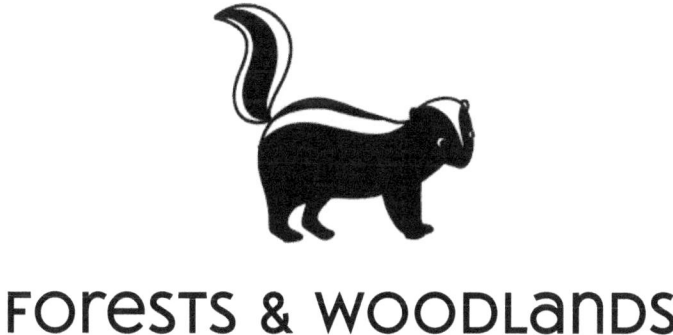

FORESTS & WOODLANDS

# raccoon

STEP 1

STEP 2

STEP 3

STEP 4

STEP 5

Done!

DRAW IT!

# SKUNK

STEP 1

STEP 2

STEP 3

STEP 4

STEP 5

DONE!

DRAW IT!

# SQUIRREL

STEP 1

STEP 2

STEP 3

STEP 4

STEP 5

Done!

DRAW IT!

# GROUNDHOG

STEP 1

STEP 2

STEP 3

STEP 4

STEP 5

DONE!

DRAW IT!

# FOX

STEP 1　　　　STEP 2　　　　STEP 3

STEP 4　　　　STEP 5　　　　Done!

Draw It!

# WOLF

STEP 1    STEP 2    STEP 3

STEP 4    STEP 5    Done!

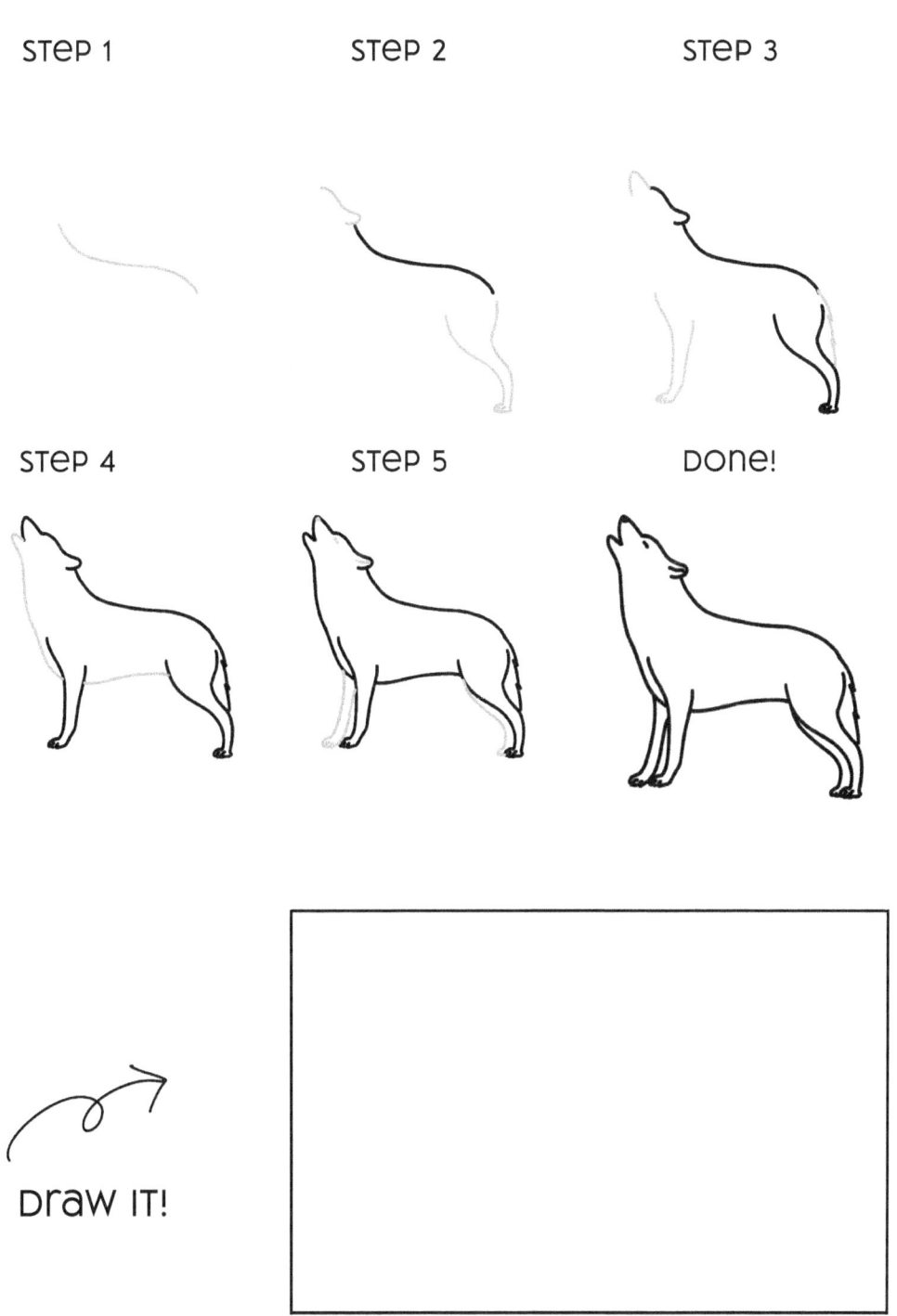

Draw it!

# mouse

STEP 1

STEP 2

STEP 3

STEP 4

STEP 5

Done!

draw it!

# RAT

STEP 1    STEP 2    STEP 3

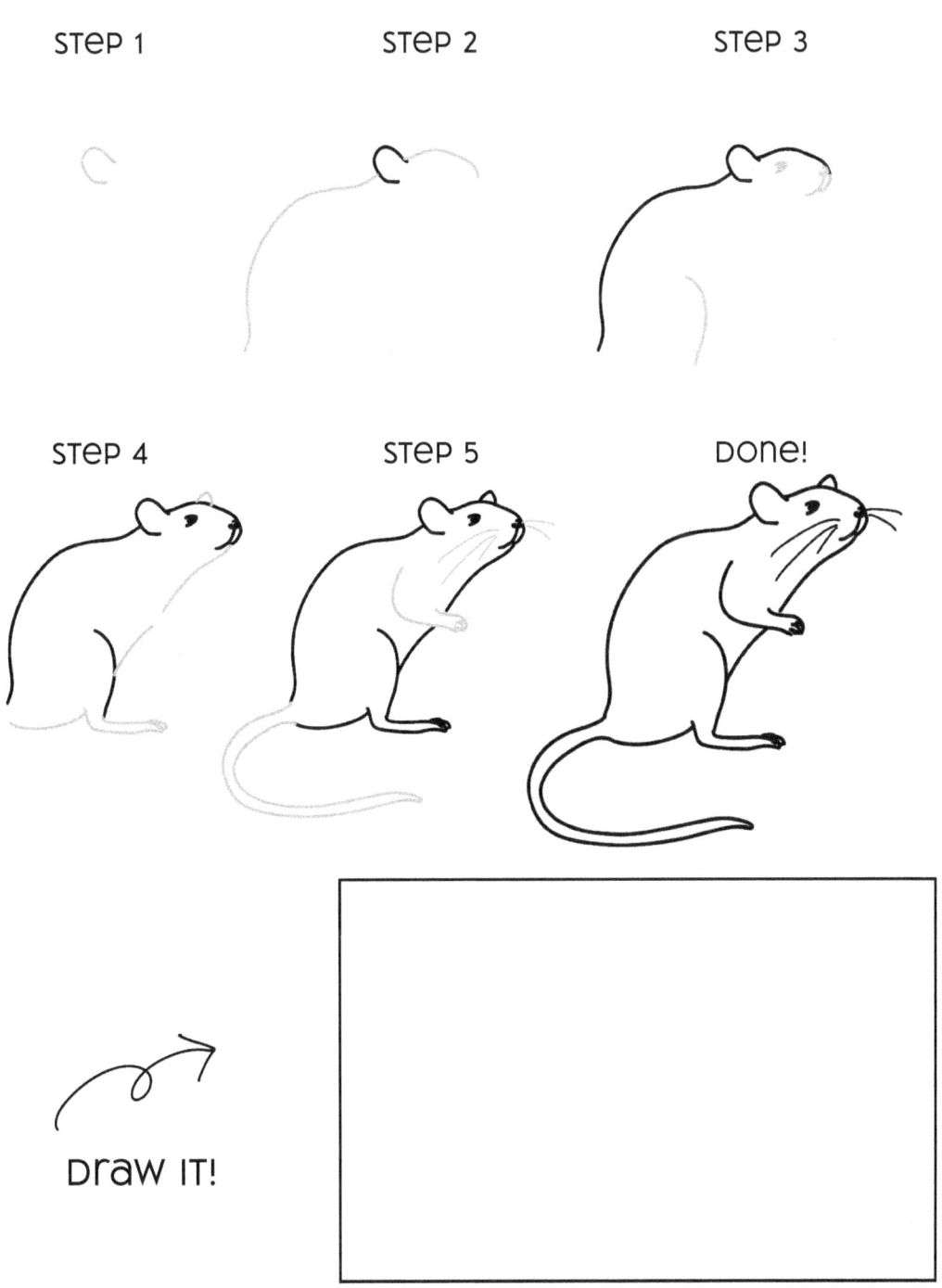

STEP 4    STEP 5    Done!

Draw it!

# Barn owl

STEP 1

STEP 2

STEP 3

STEP 4

STEP 5

Done!

Draw it!

# great Horned OWL

STEP 1　　　　STEP 2　　　　STEP 3

STEP 4　　　　STEP 5　　　　Done!

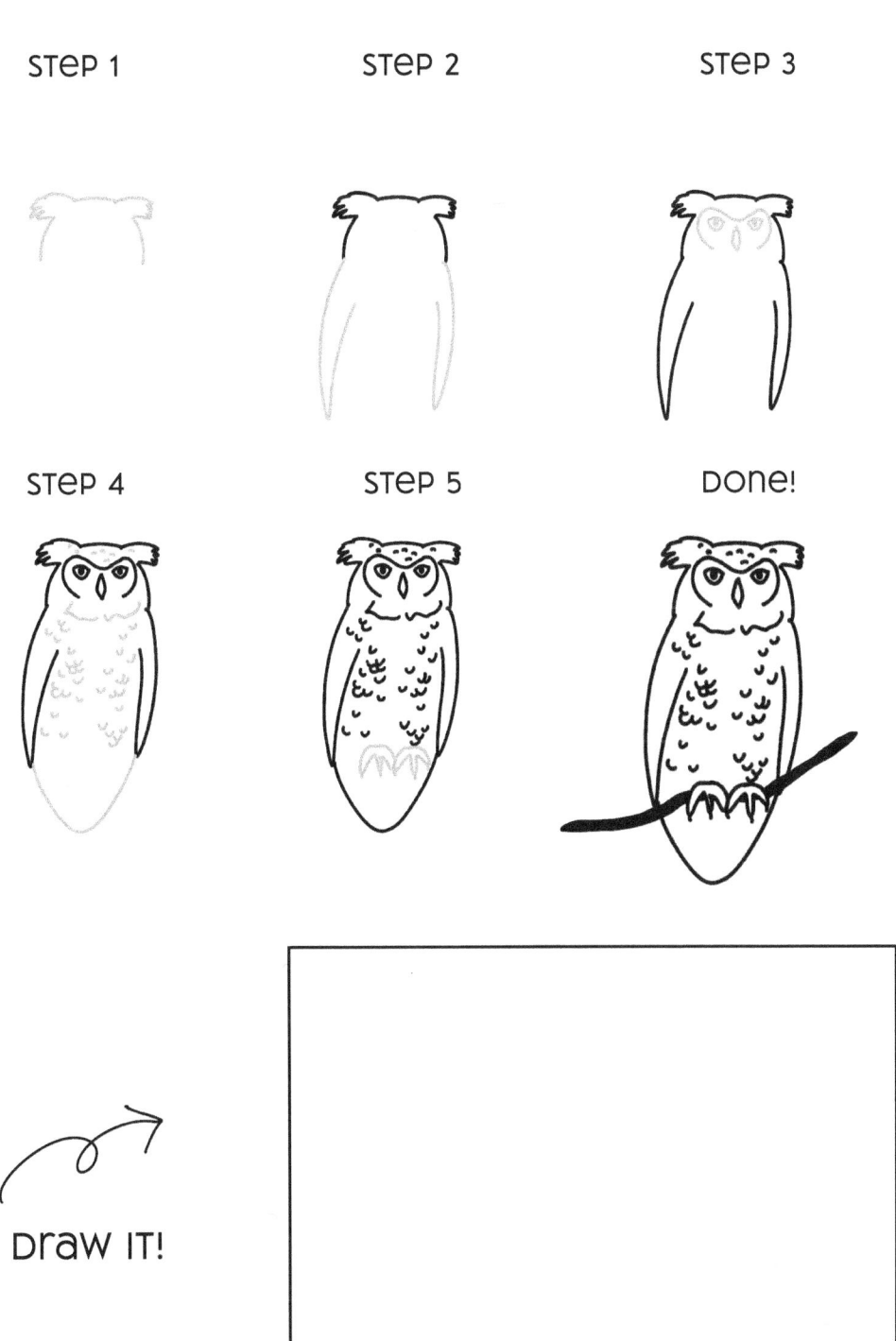

DRAW IT!

# SCREECH OWL

STEP 1  STEP 2  STEP 3

STEP 4  STEP 5  Done!

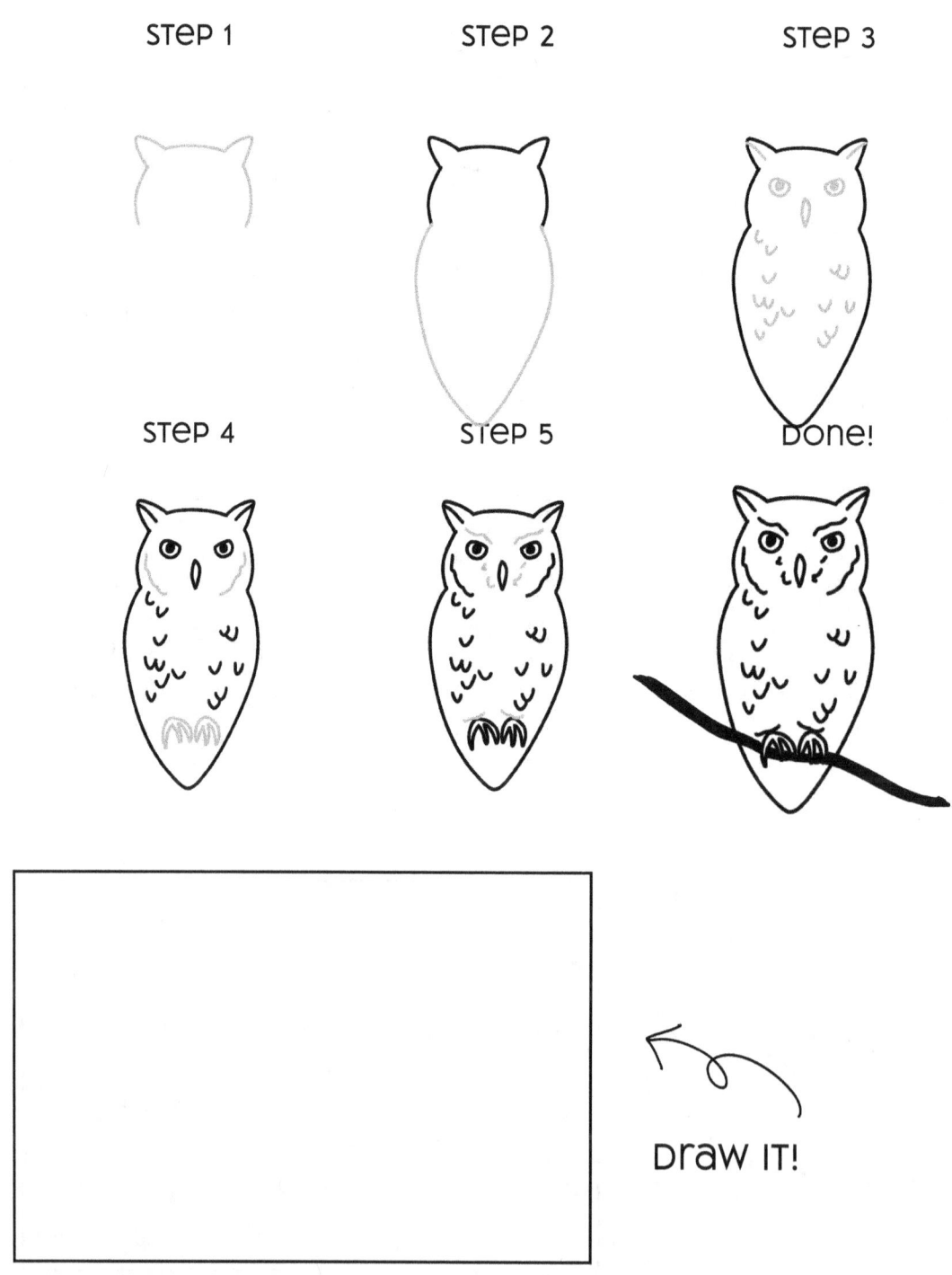

DRAW IT!

# woodpecker

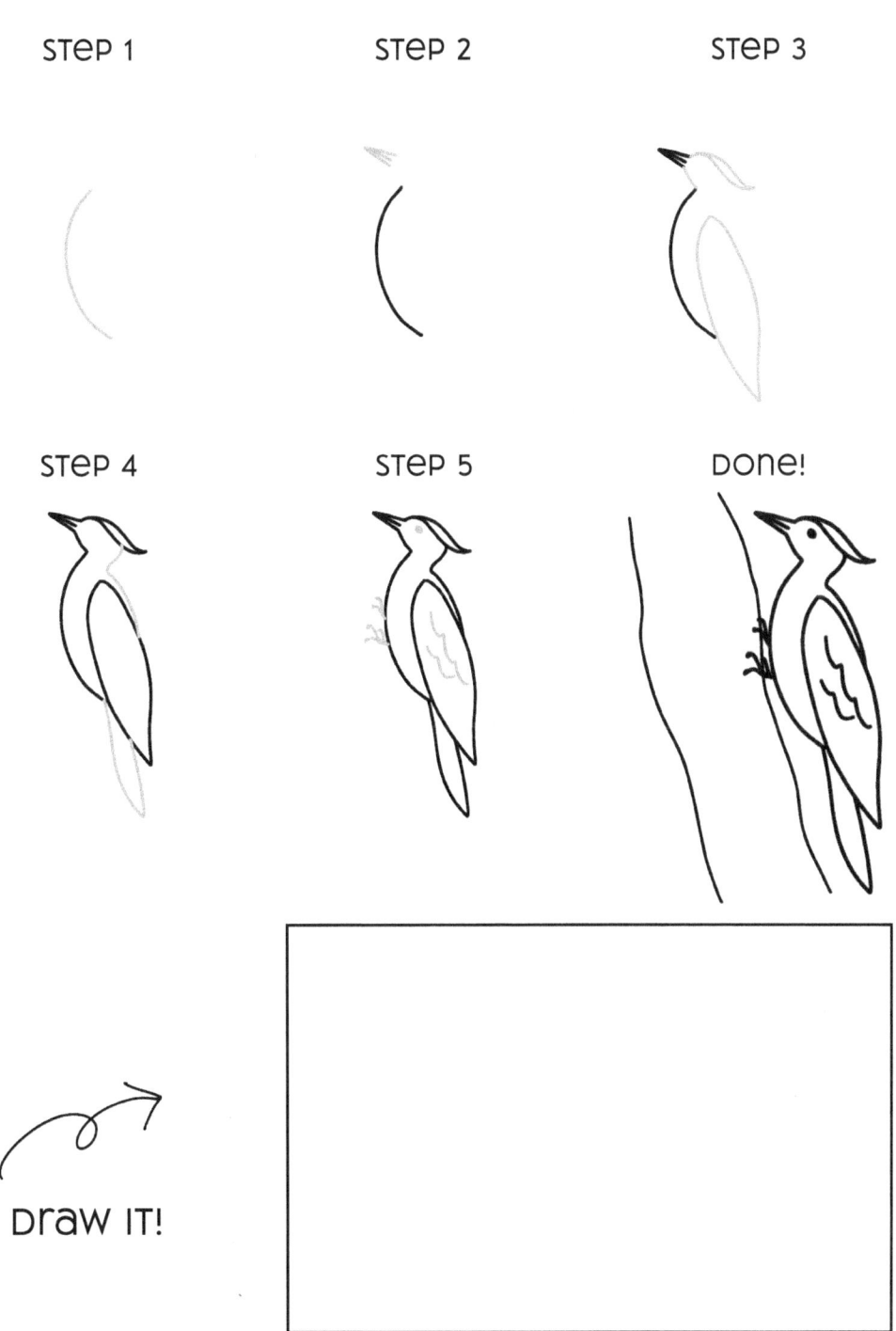

STEP 1

STEP 2

STEP 3

STEP 4

STEP 5

Done!

Draw it!

# HUMMINGBIRD

STEP 1

STEP 2

STEP 3

STEP 4

STEP 5

DONE!

DRAW IT!

# armaDILLo

STEP 1

STEP 2

STEP 3

STEP 4

STEP 5

Done!

Draw IT!

# koala

STEP 1 STEP 2 STEP 3

STEP 4 STEP 5 Done!

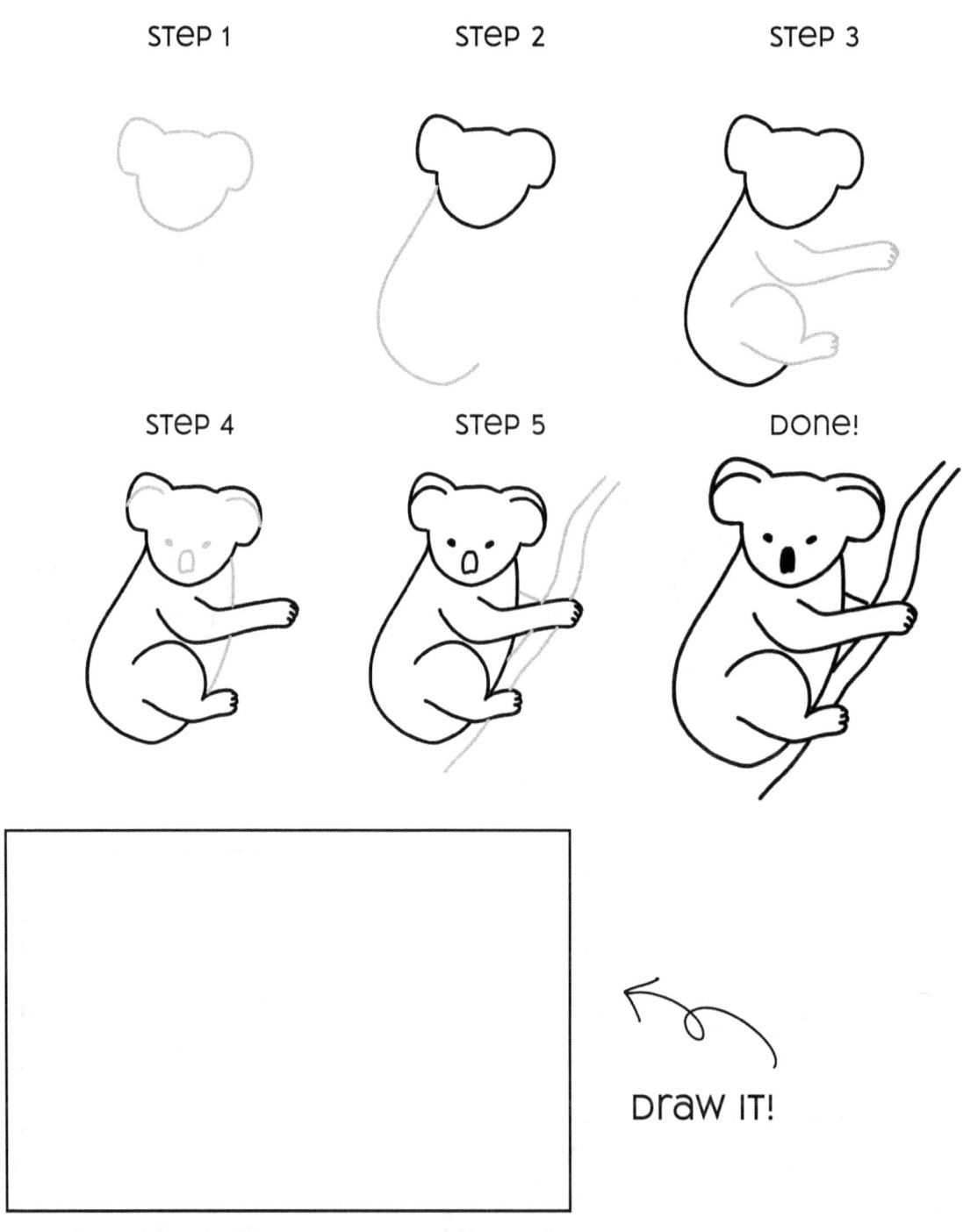

Draw IT!

next up... meadows

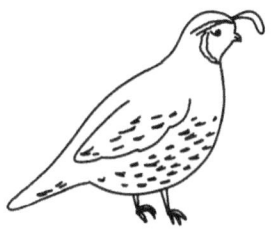

meaDOWS

# rabbit

STEP 1      STEP 2      STEP 3

STEP 4      STEP 5      Done!

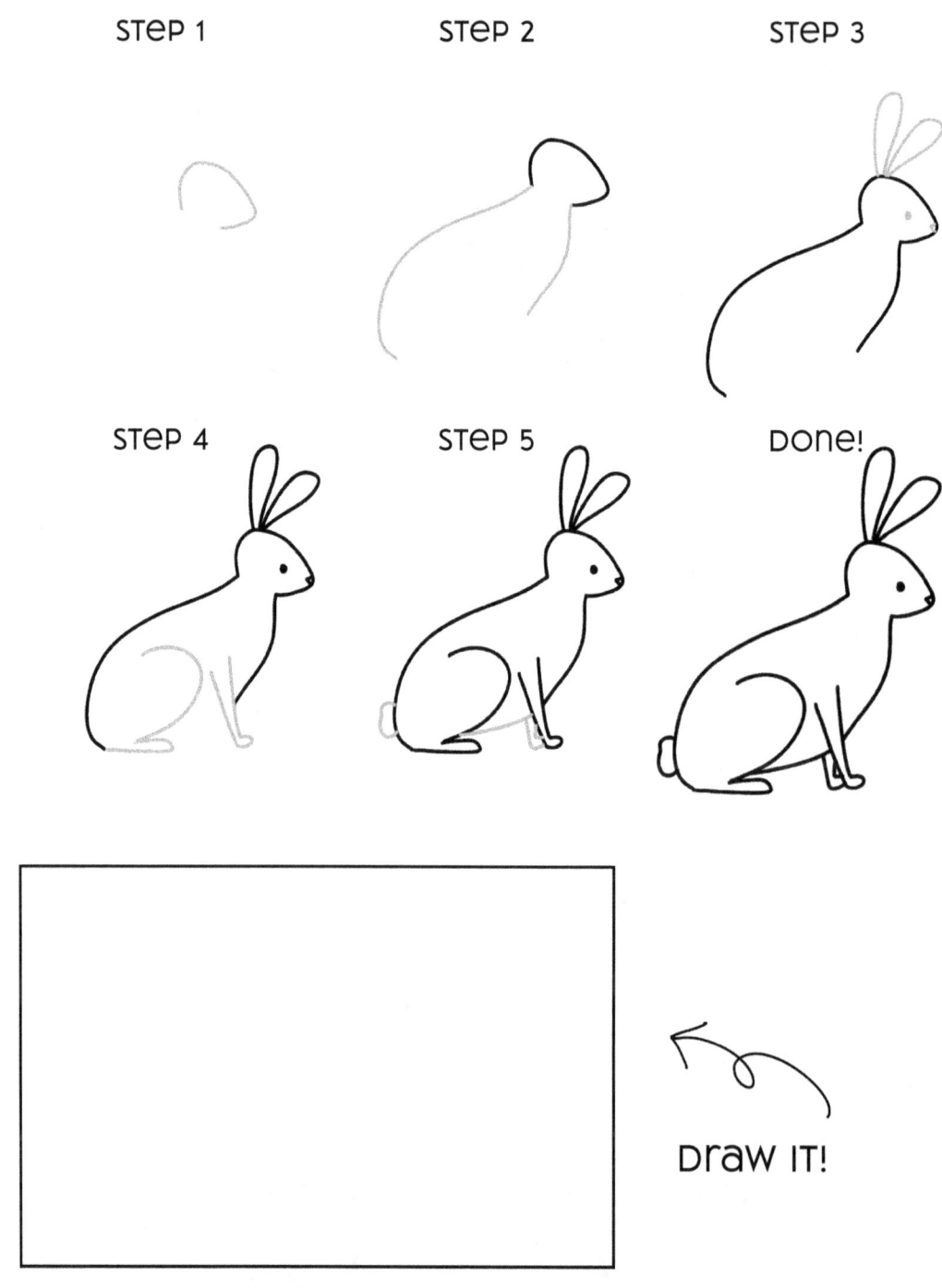

DRAW IT!

meaDOWS

# HEDGEHOG

STEP 1

STEP 2

STEP 3

STEP 4

STEP 5

DONE!

DRAW IT!

# weasel

STEP 1

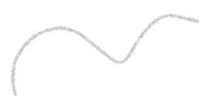

STEP 2

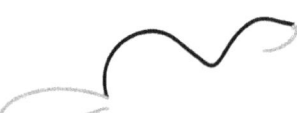

STEP 3

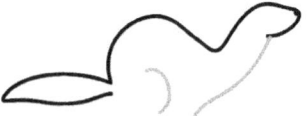

STEP 4

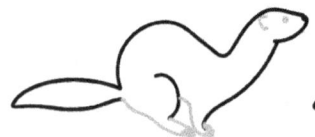

STEP 5

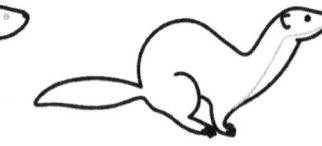

Done!

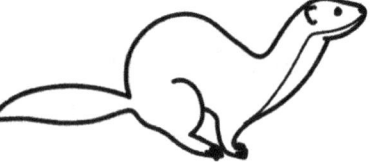

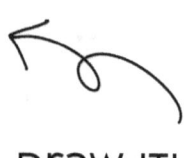

Draw it!

meadows

# sable

STEP 1

STEP 2

STEP 3

STEP 4

STEP 5

DONE!

DRAW IT!

# mole

STEP 1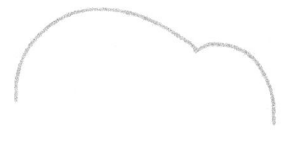

STEP 2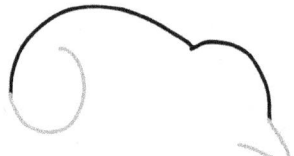

STEP 3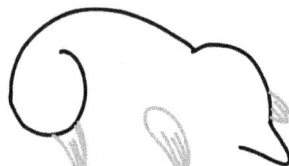

STEP 4

STEP 5

Done!

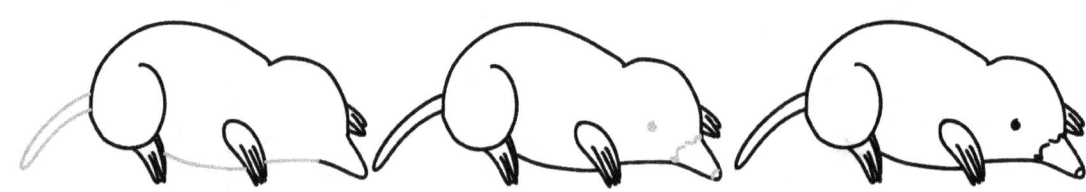

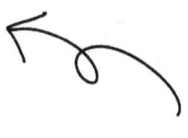

Draw It!

# OPOSSUM

STEP 1             STEP 2             STEP 3

STEP 4             STEP 5             DONE!

DRAW IT!

# CHICKEN

STEP 1

STEP 2

STEP 3

STEP 4

STEP 5

Done!

Draw IT!

# rooster

STEP 1 STEP 2 STEP 3

STEP 4 STEP 5 DONE!

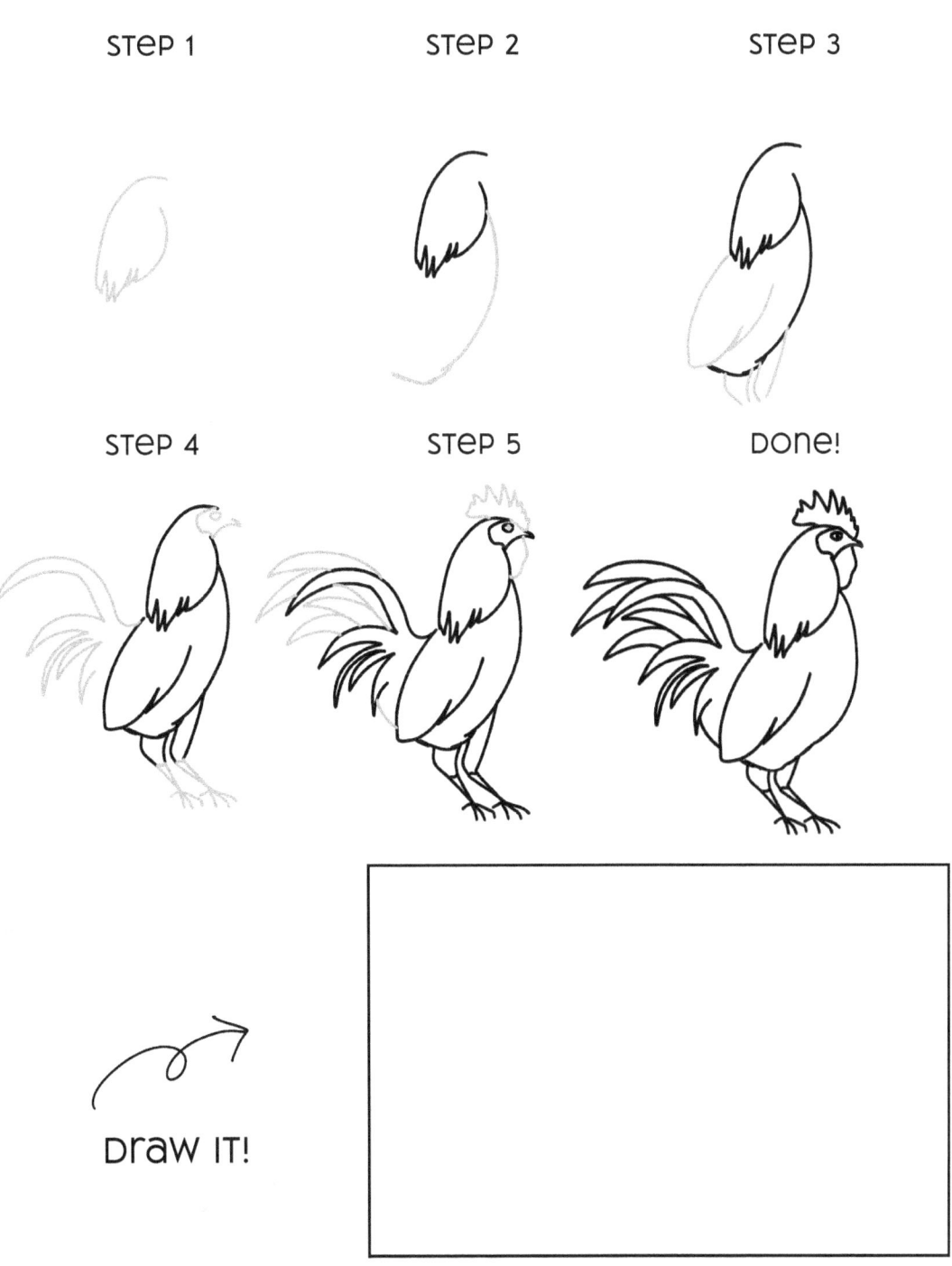

DRAW IT!

# QUAIL

STEP 1

STEP 2

STEP 3

STEP 4

STEP 5

Done!

Draw it!

meadows

# turkey

STEP 1

STEP 2

STEP 3

STEP 4

STEP 5

done!

draw it!

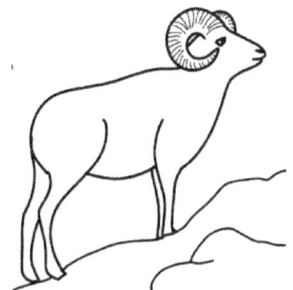

mountains

# ram

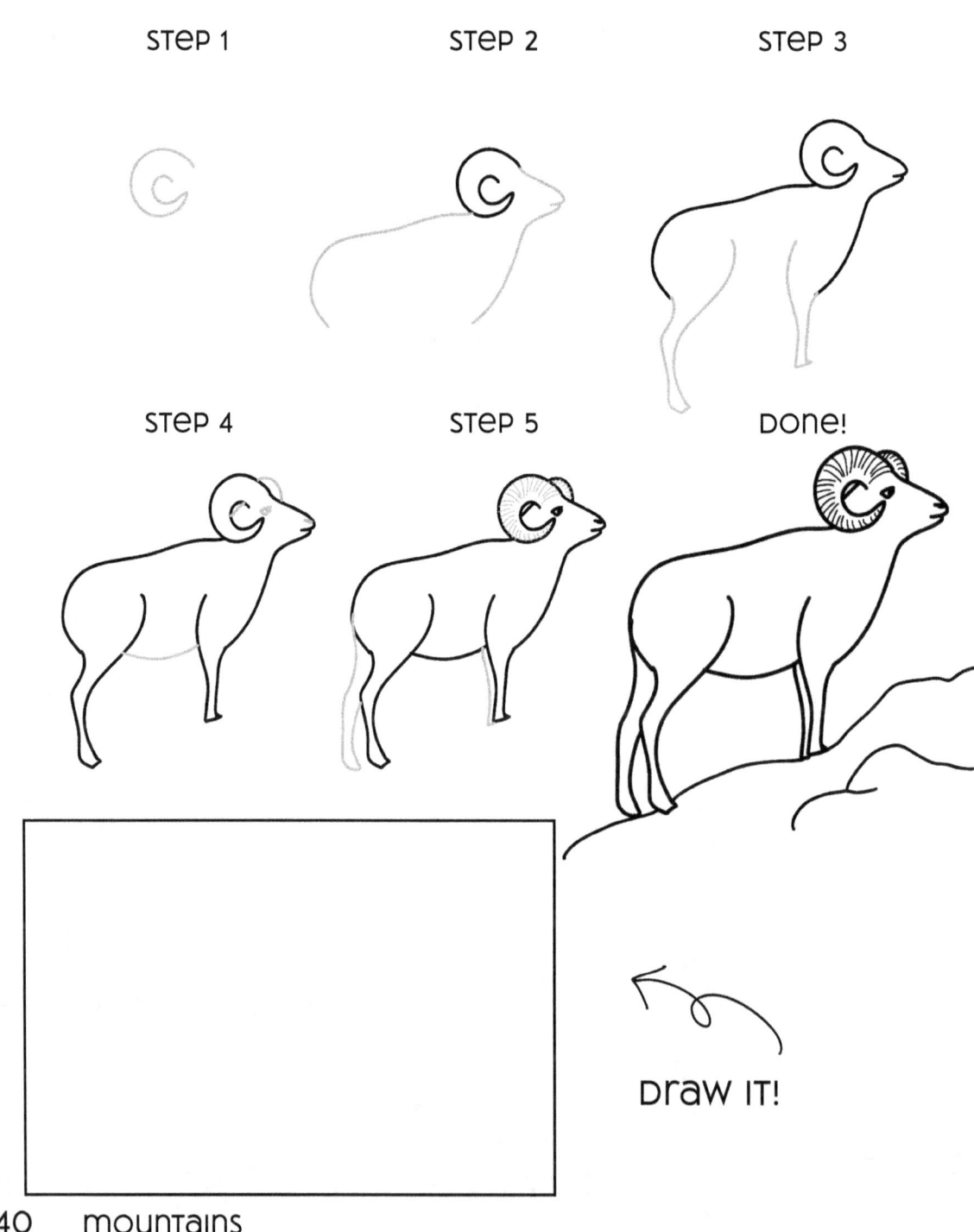

STEP 1

STEP 2

STEP 3

STEP 4

STEP 5

Done!

Draw it!

40    mountains

# SHEEP

STEP 1    STEP 2    STEP 3

STEP 4    STEP 5    DONE!

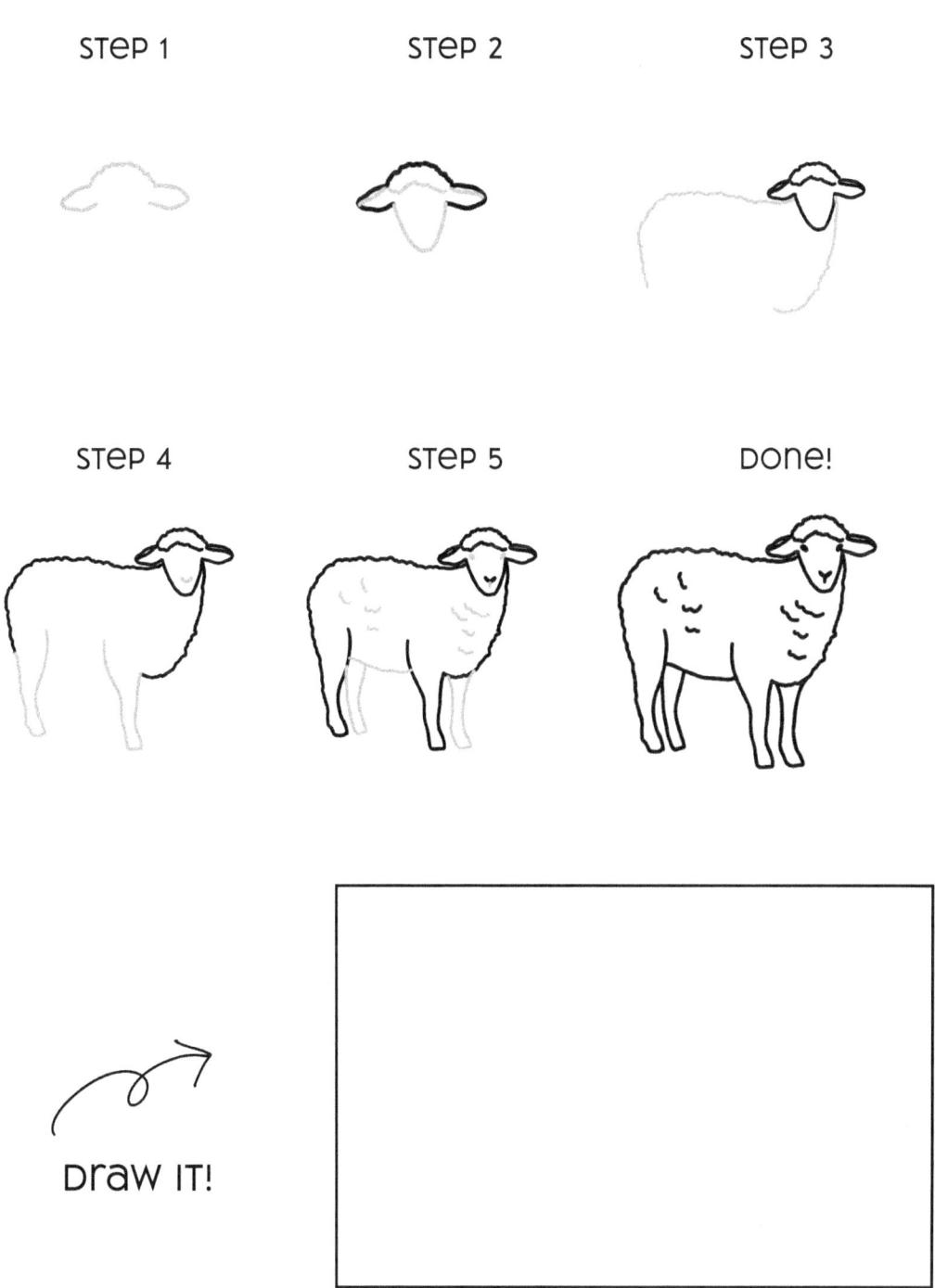

DRAW IT!

# LLama

STEP 1

STEP 2

STEP 3

STEP 4

STEP 5

Done!

Draw it!

mountains

# GOAT

STEP 1

STEP 2

STEP 3

STEP 4

STEP 5

DONE!

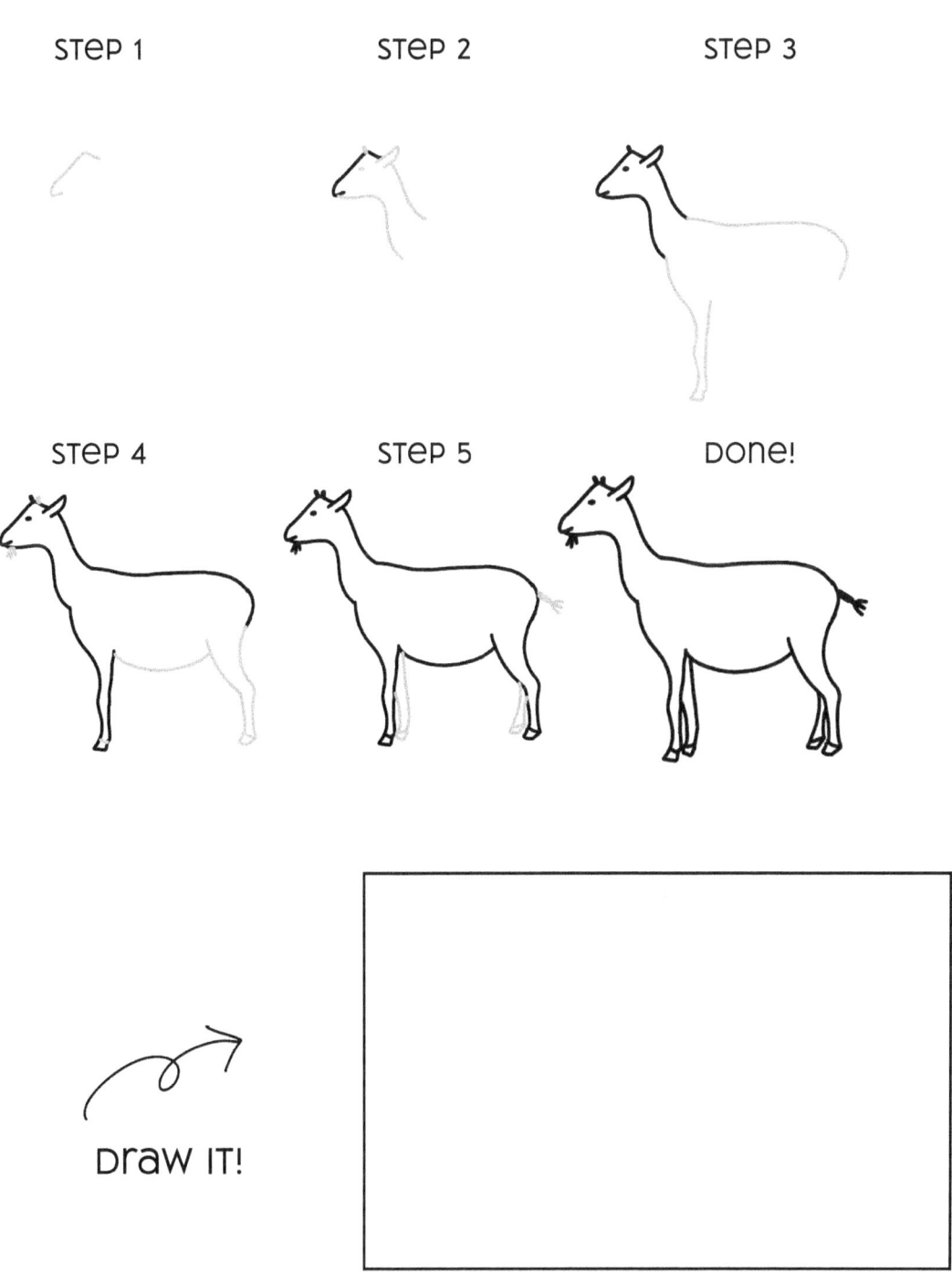

DRAW IT!

# HIGHLAND CATTLE

STEP 1

STEP 2

STEP 3

STEP 4

STEP 5

Done!

DRAW IT!

mountains

next up... Prairies & Plains

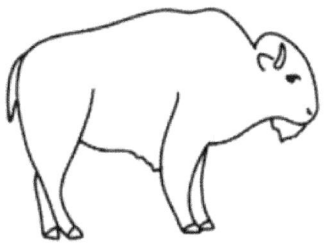

# Prairies & Plains

# Horse

STEP 1

STEP 2

STEP 3

STEP 4

STEP 5

Done!

DRAW IT!

# BISON

STEP 1    STEP 2    STEP 3

STEP 4    STEP 5    Done!

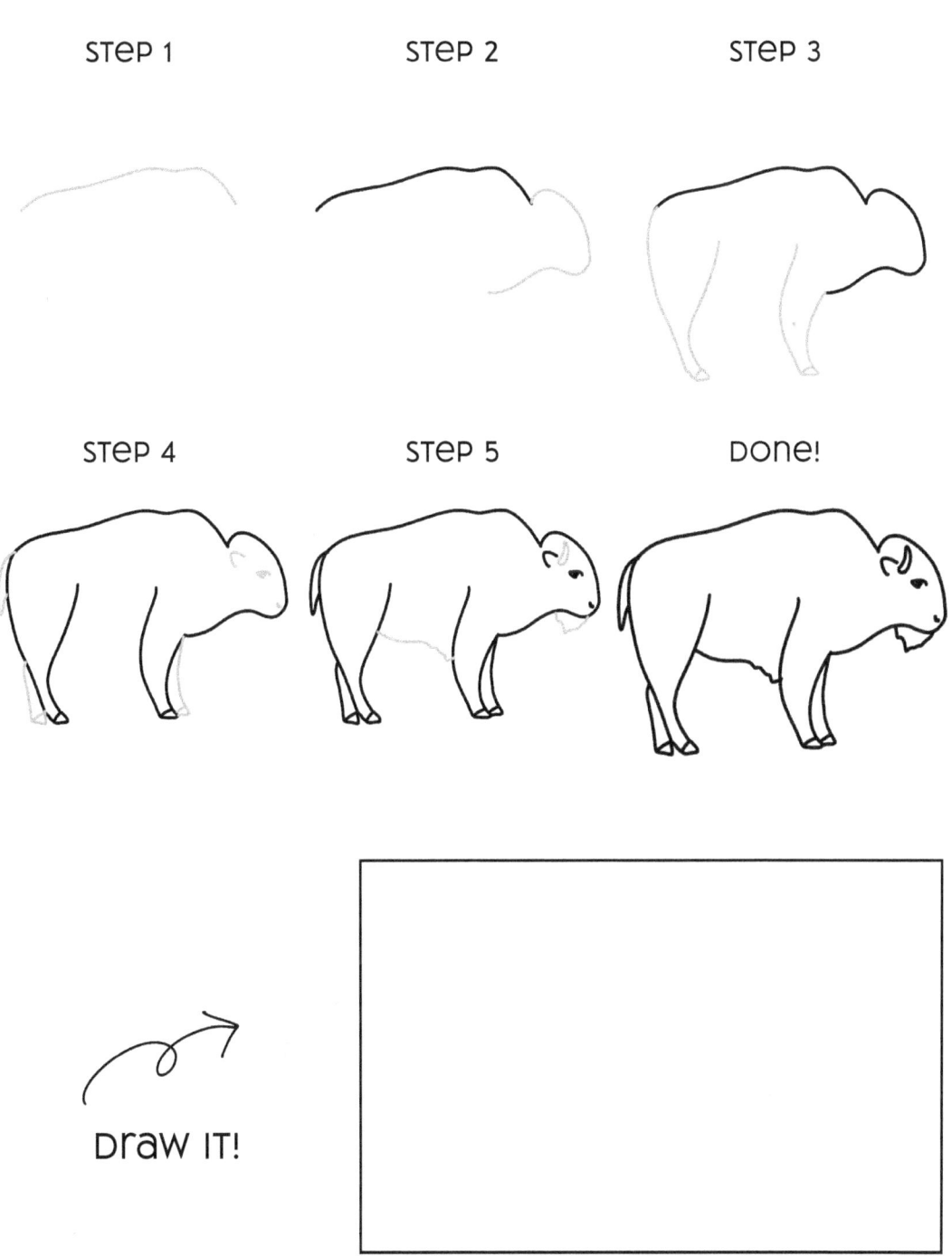

Draw it!

# BaDGer

STEP 1          STEP 2          STEP 3

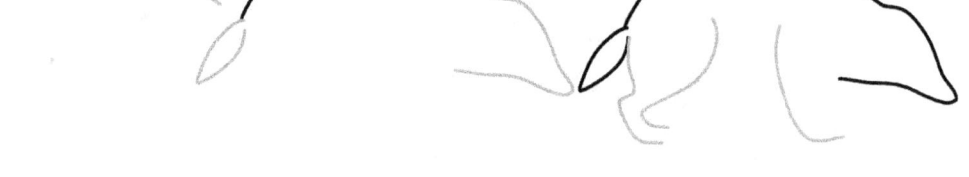

STEP 4          STEP 5          Done!

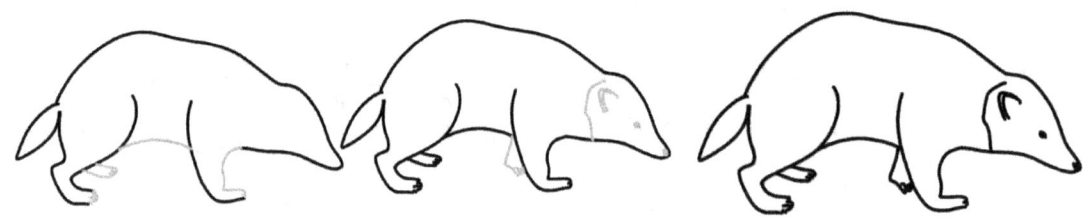

Draw IT!

# SNOWY OWL

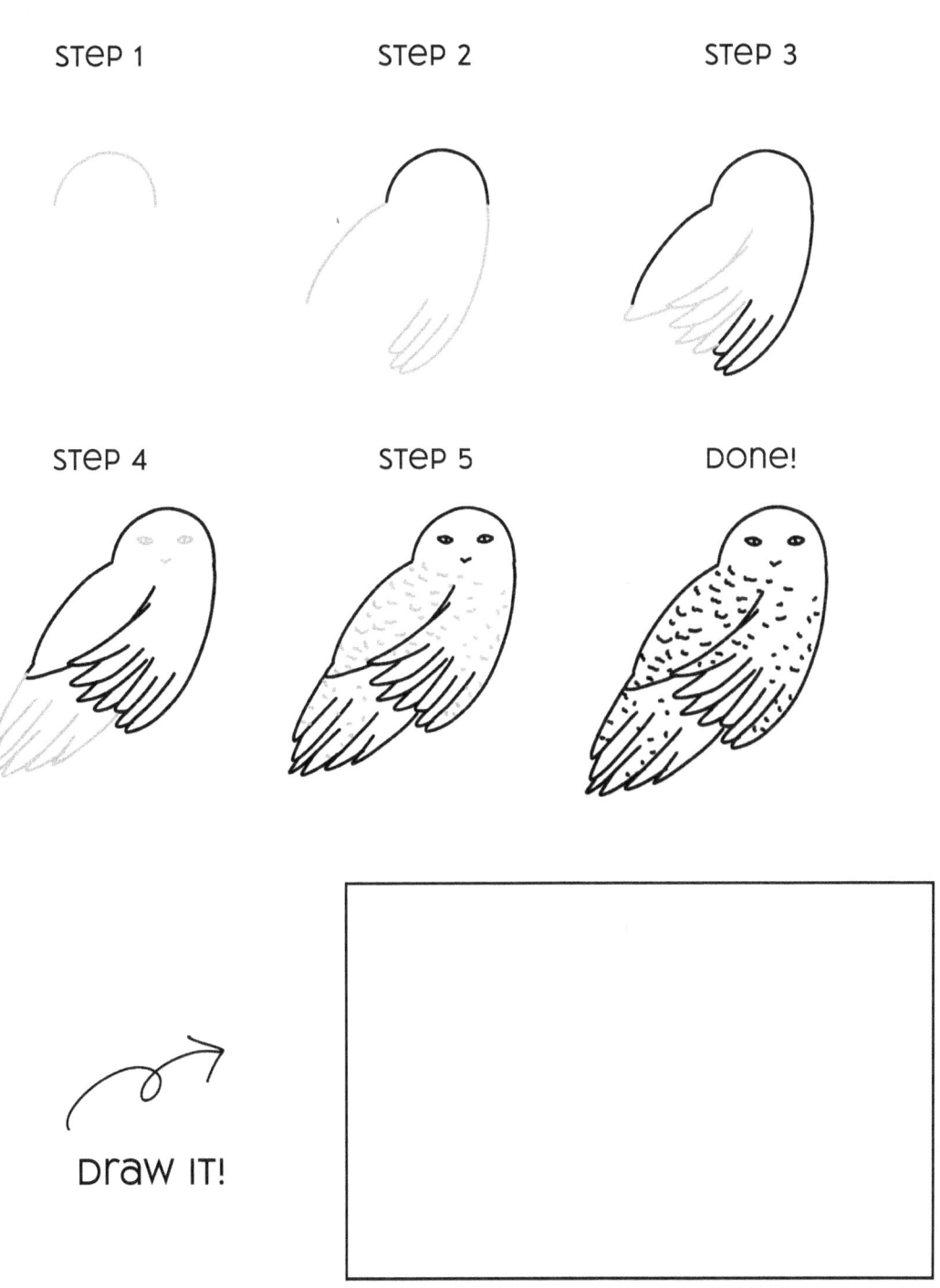

STEP 1

STEP 2

STEP 3

STEP 4

STEP 5

Done!

Draw it!

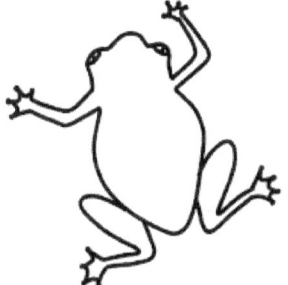

# Rivers, Marshes, & Lakes

# Beaver

STEP 1

STEP 2

STEP 3

STEP 4

STEP 5

Done!

Draw It!

rivers, marshes, & lakes

# otter

STEP 1

STEP 2

STEP 3

STEP 4

STEP 5

Done!

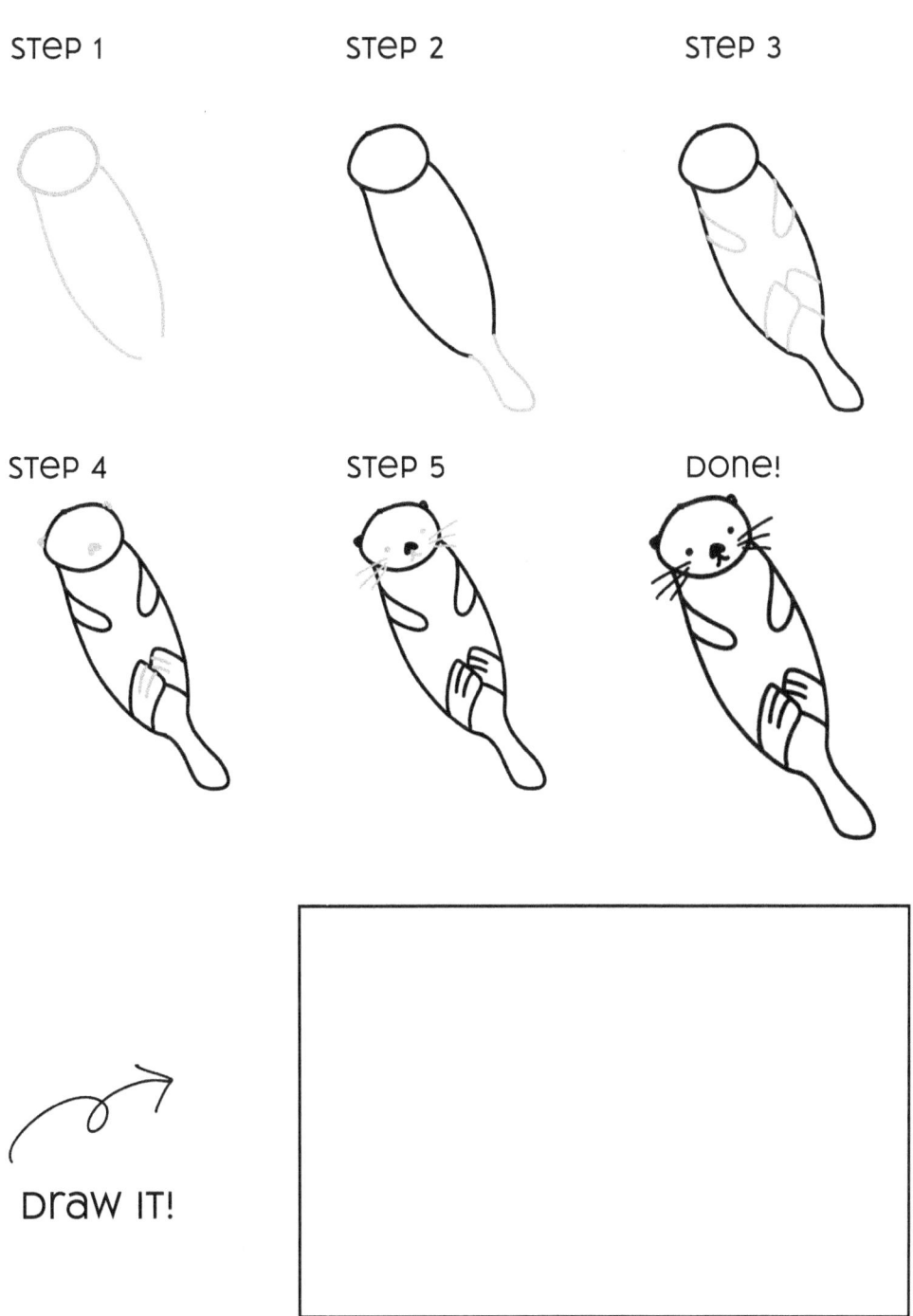

Draw it!

# alligator

STEP 1

STEP 2

STEP 3

STEP 4

STEP 5

Done!

DRAW IT!

rivers, marshes, & lakes

# PLATYPUS

STEP 1

STEP 2

STEP 3

STEP 4

STEP 5

Done!

DRAW IT!

# snail

STEP 1        STEP 2        STEP 3

STEP 4        STEP 5        Done!

Draw IT!

rivers, marshes, & lakes

# Frog

STEP 1

STEP 2

STEP 3

STEP 4

STEP 5

Done!

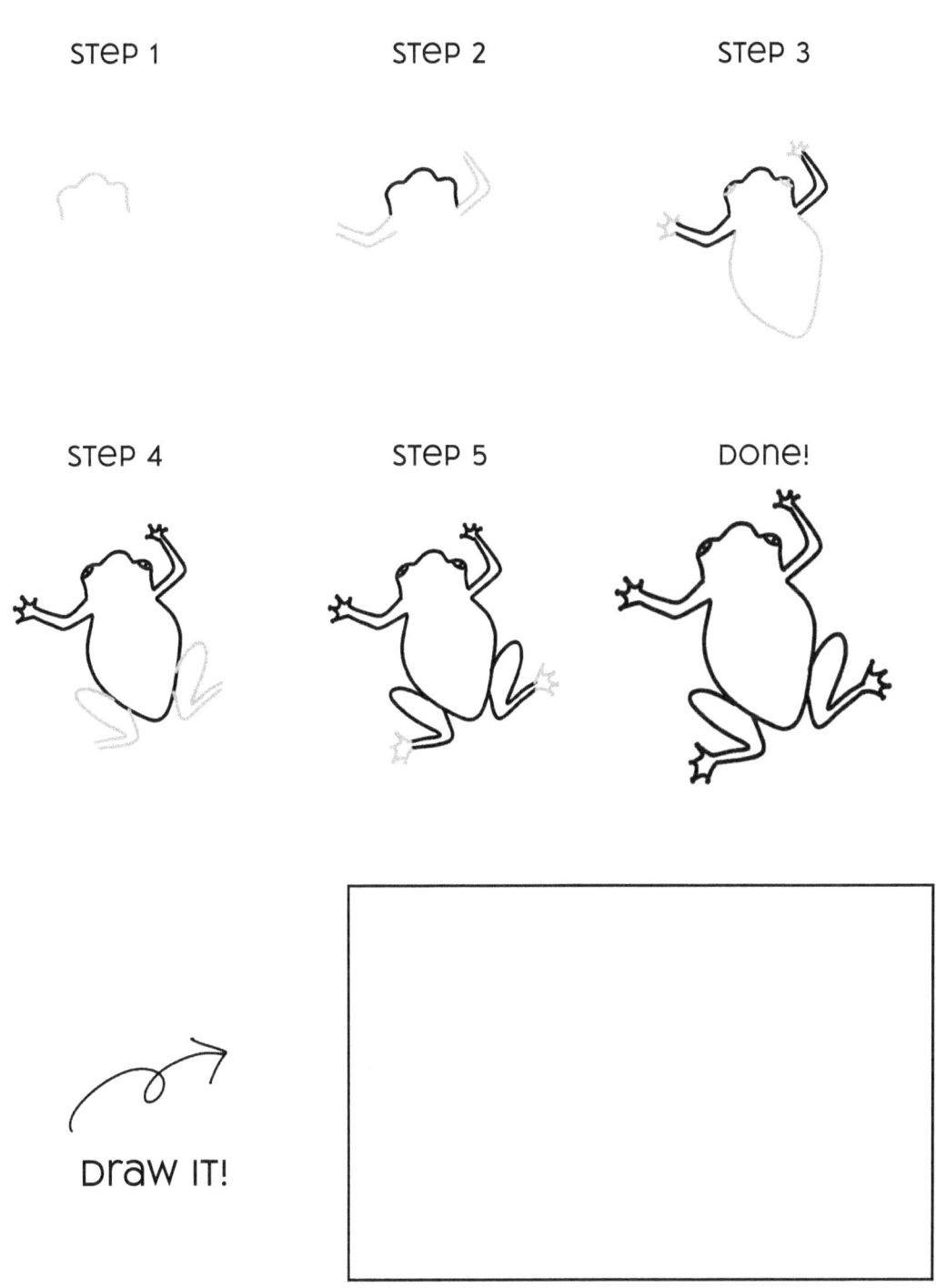

Draw IT!

# GOLDFISH

STEP 1          STEP 2          STEP 3

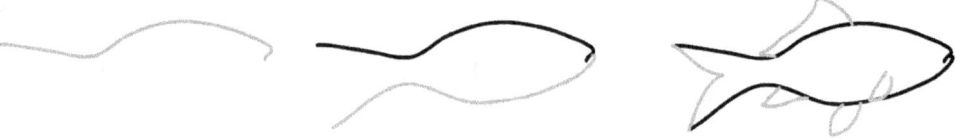

STEP 4          STEP 5          DONE!v

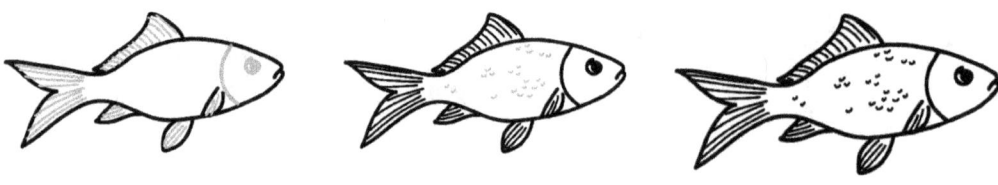

DRAW IT!

# BETTA FISH

STEP 1

STEP 2

STEP 3

STEP 4

STEP 5

Done!

Draw it!

rivers, marshes, & lakes

# salmon

STEP 1       STEP 2       STEP 3

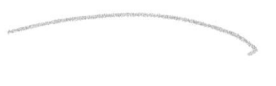  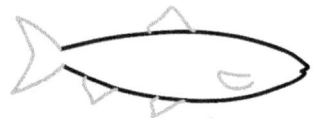

STEP 4       STEP 5       Done!

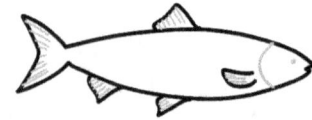 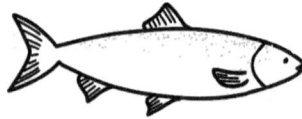 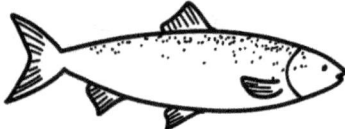

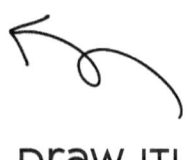

DRAW IT!

rivers, marshes, & lakes

# moose

STEP 1    STEP 2    STEP 3

STEP 4    STEP 5    Done!

DRAW IT!

# HIPPOPOTAMUS

STEP 1

STEP 2

STEP 3

STEP 4

STEP 5

Done!

DRAW IT!

# Quokka

STEP 1    STEP 2    STEP 3

STEP 4    STEP 5    Done!

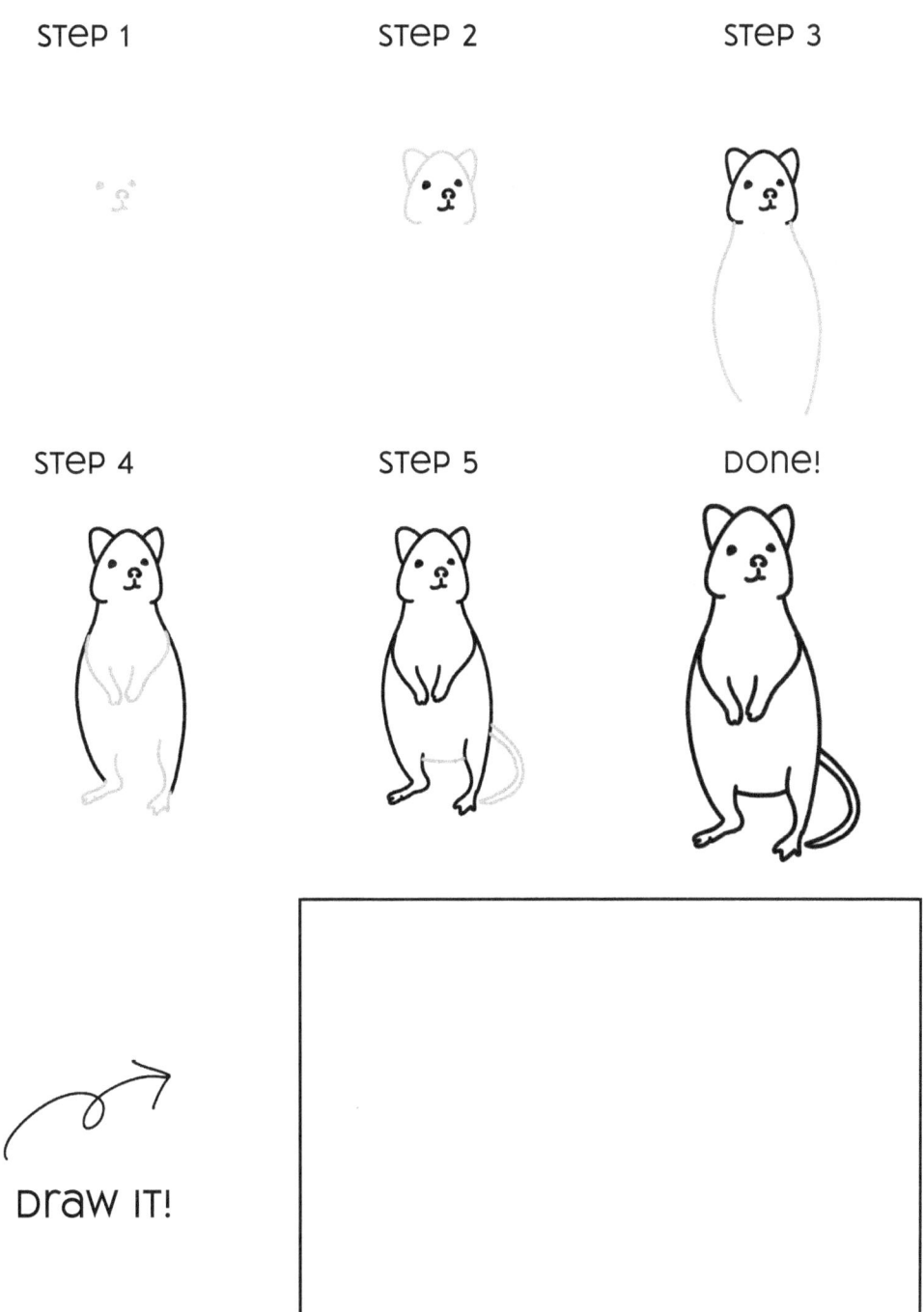

Draw it!

# STORK

STEP 1

STEP 2

STEP 3

STEP 4

STEP 5

Done!

Draw IT!

# FLAMINGO

STEP 1

STEP 2

STEP 3

STEP 4

STEP 5

DONE!

DRAW IT!

# Heron

STEP 1

STEP 2

STEP 3

STEP 4

STEP 5

DONE!

DRAW IT!

# PHEASANT

STEP 1     STEP 2     STEP 3

STEP 4     STEP 5     Done!

Draw IT!

# GOOSE

STEP 1      STEP 2      STEP 3

STEP 4      STEP 5      Done!

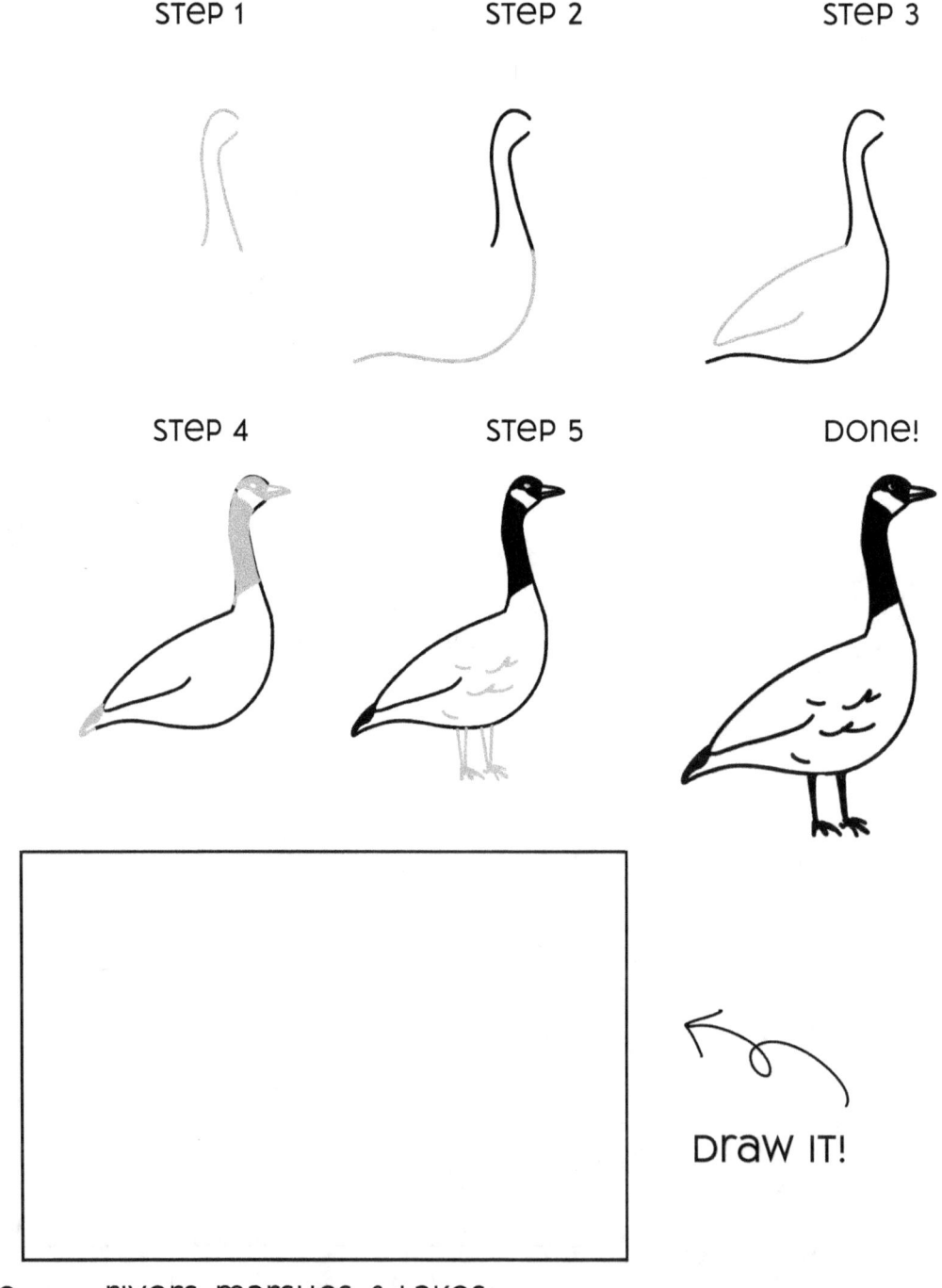

Draw it!

rivers, marshes, & lakes

# swan

STEP 1         STEP 2         STEP 3

STEP 4         STEP 5         Done!

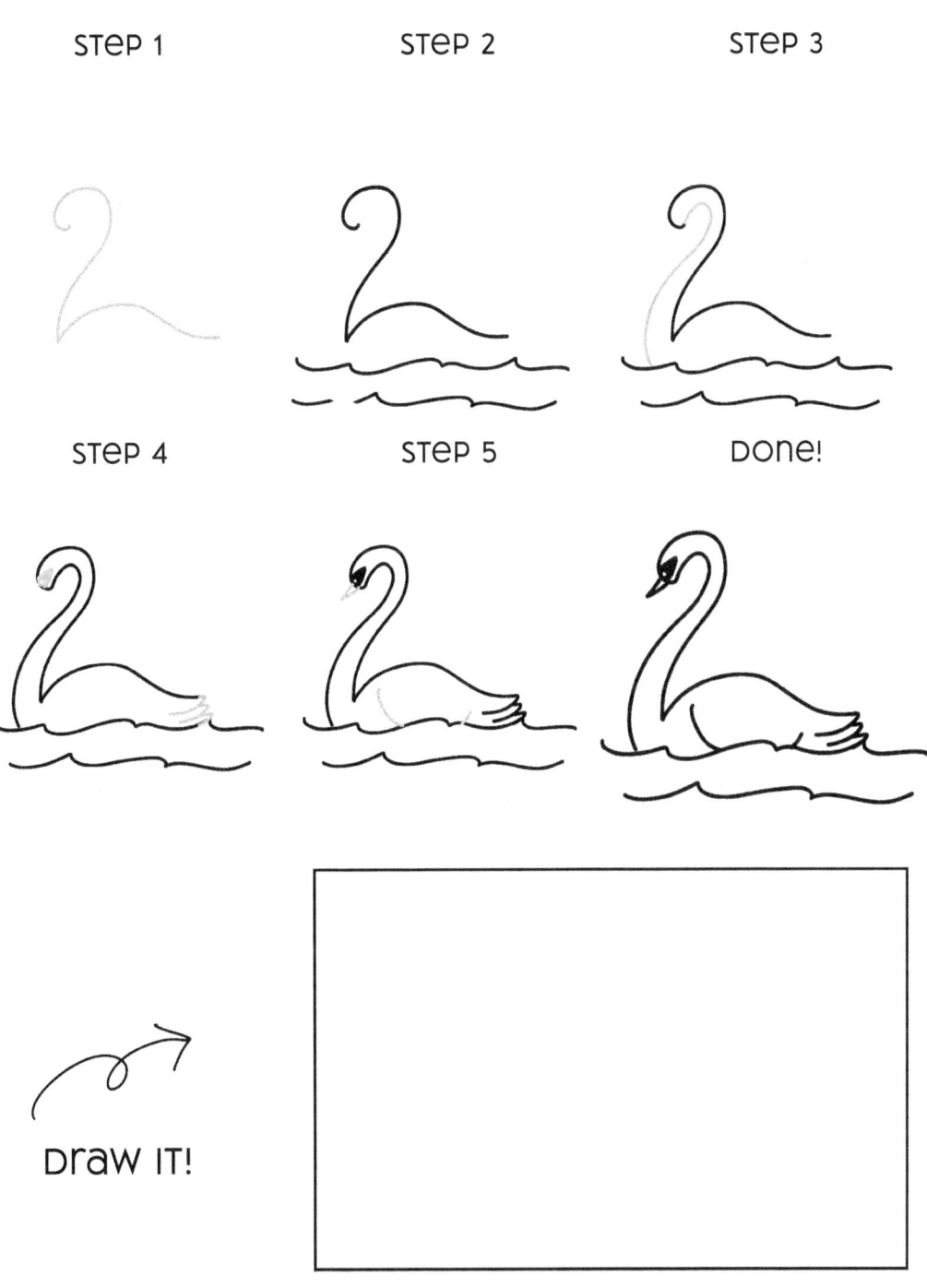

Draw it!

# DUCK

STEP 1

STEP 2

STEP 3

STEP 4

STEP 5

Done!

Draw IT!

rivers, marshes, & Lakes

V

STEP 1          STEP 2          STEP 3

STEP 4          STEP 5          Done!

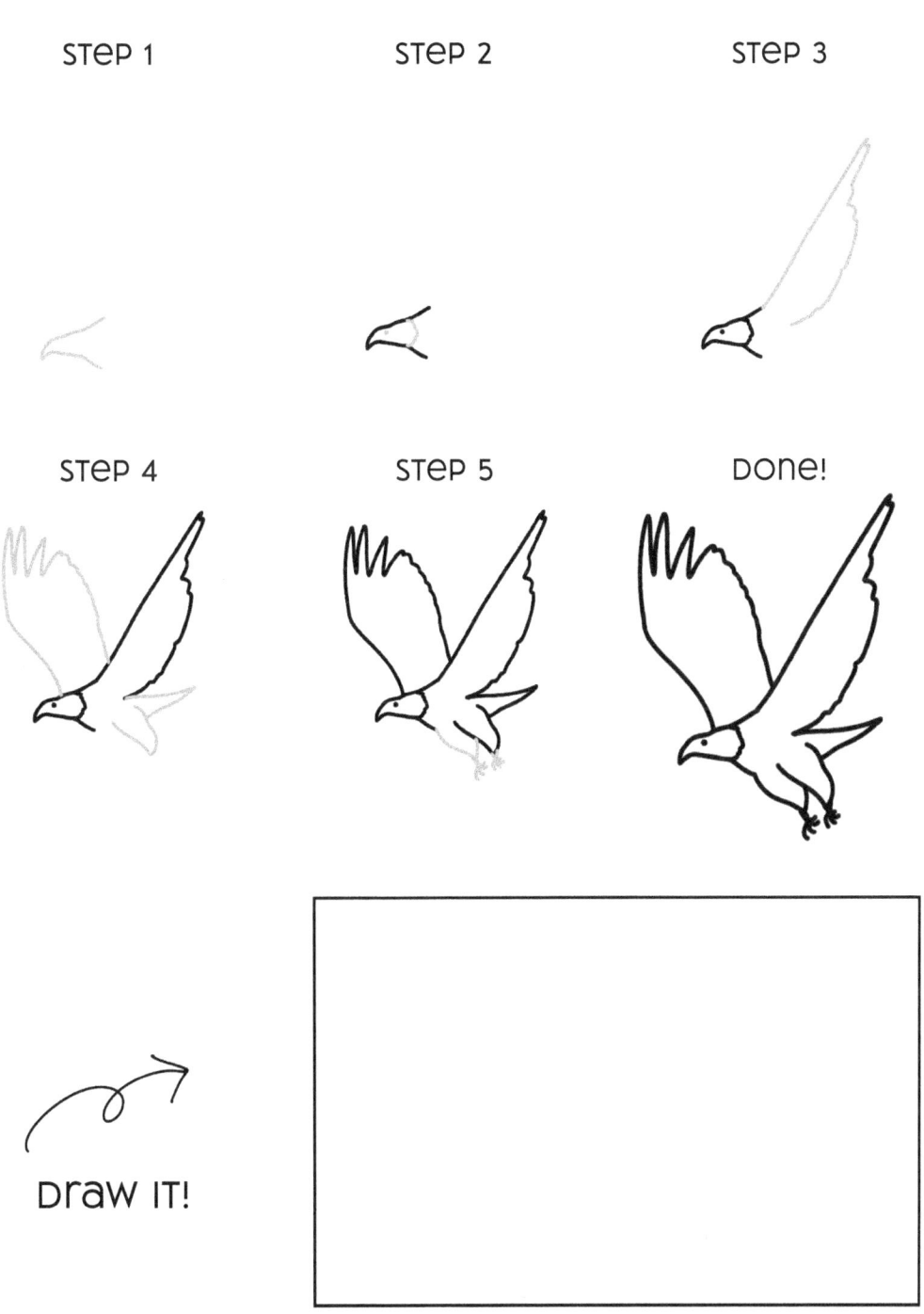

Draw it!

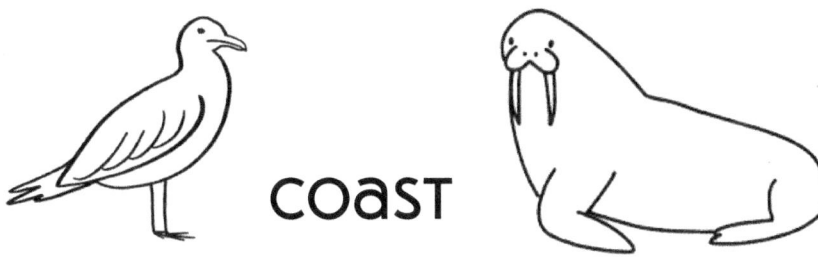

coast

# walrus

STEP 1

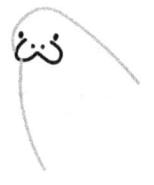

STEP 2

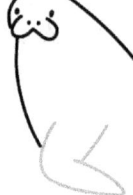

STEP 3

STEP 4

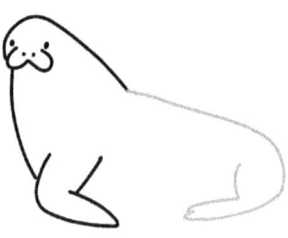

STEP 5

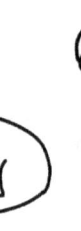
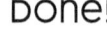

Done!

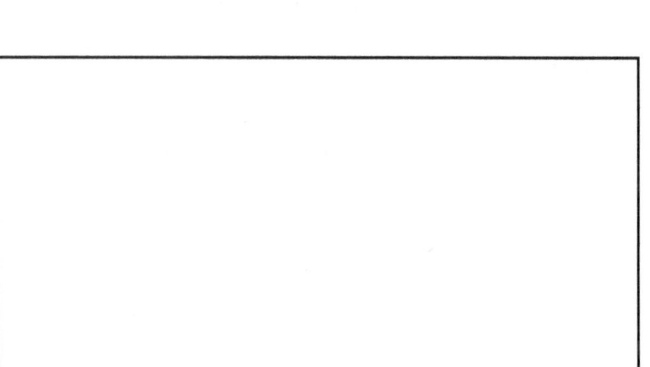

Draw it!

coast

# FALCON

STEP 1     STEP 2     STEP 3

STEP 4     STEP 5     DONE!

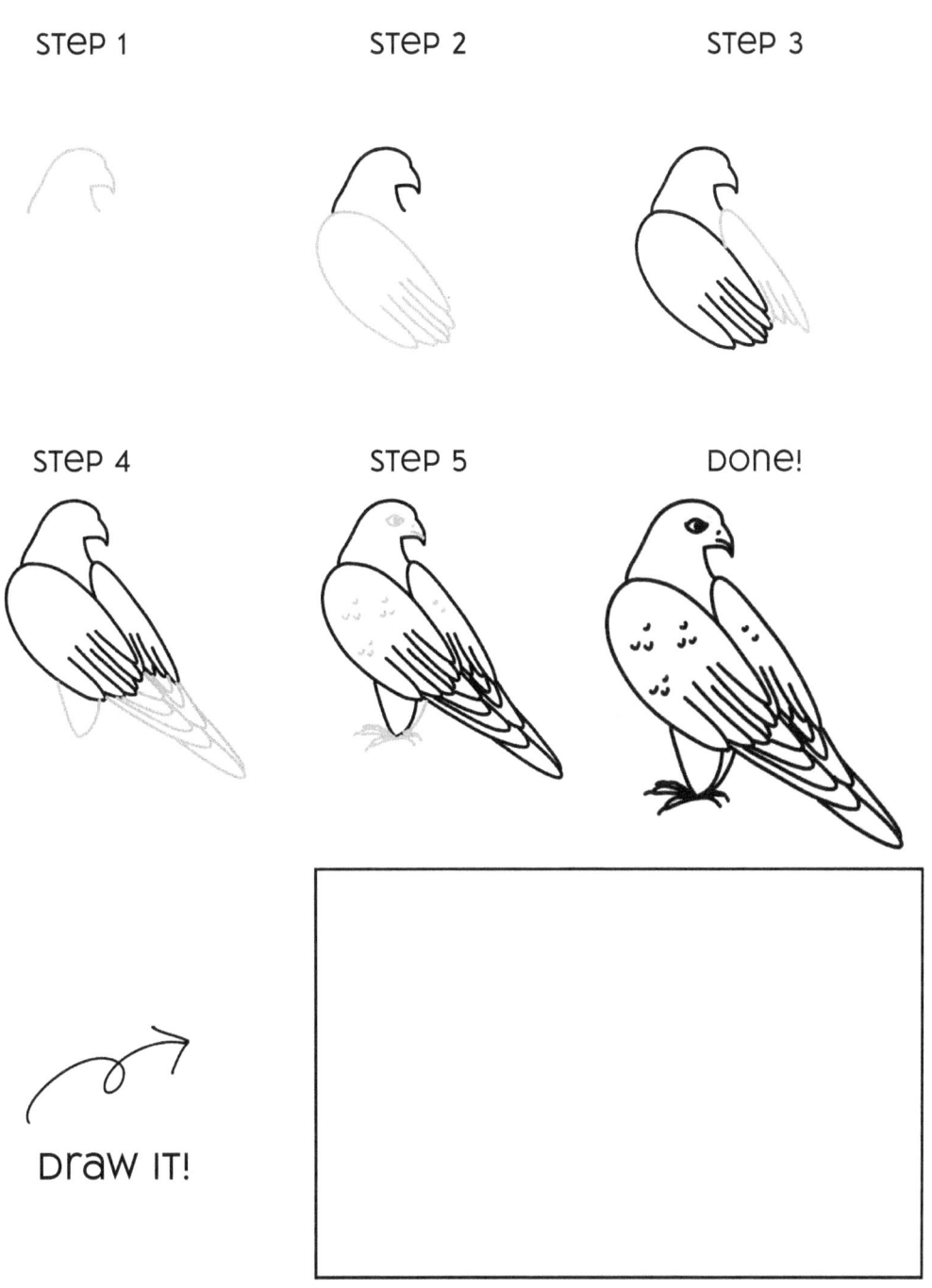

Draw IT!

# seagull

STEP 1          STEP 2          STEP 3

STEP 4          STEP 5          Done!

Draw it!

coast

# ALBATROSS

STEP 1

STEP 2

STEP 3

STEP 4

STEP 5

DONE!

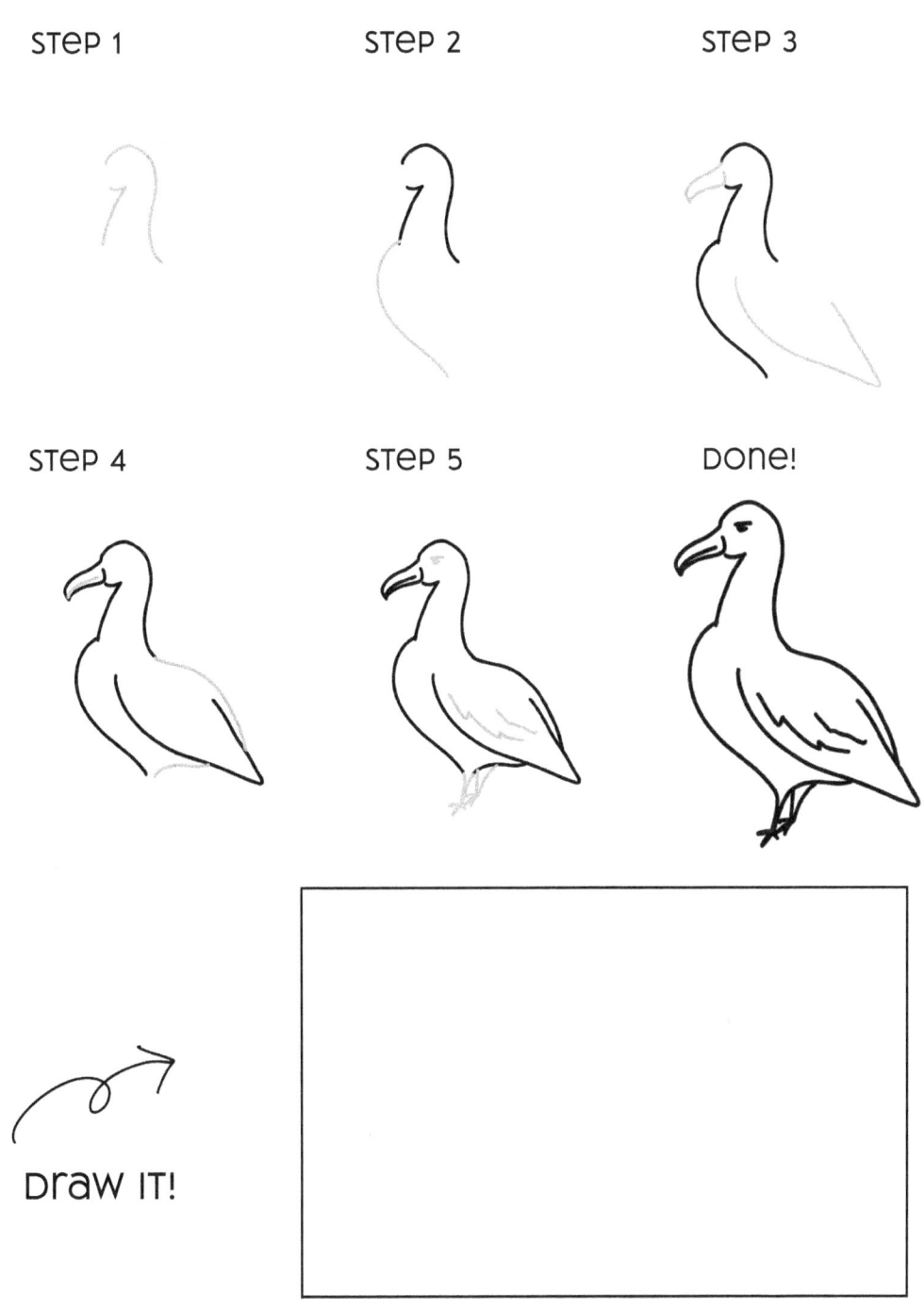

DRAW IT!

# PUFFIN

STEP 1　　　　STEP 2　　　　STEP 3

STEP 4　　　　STEP 5　　　　Done!

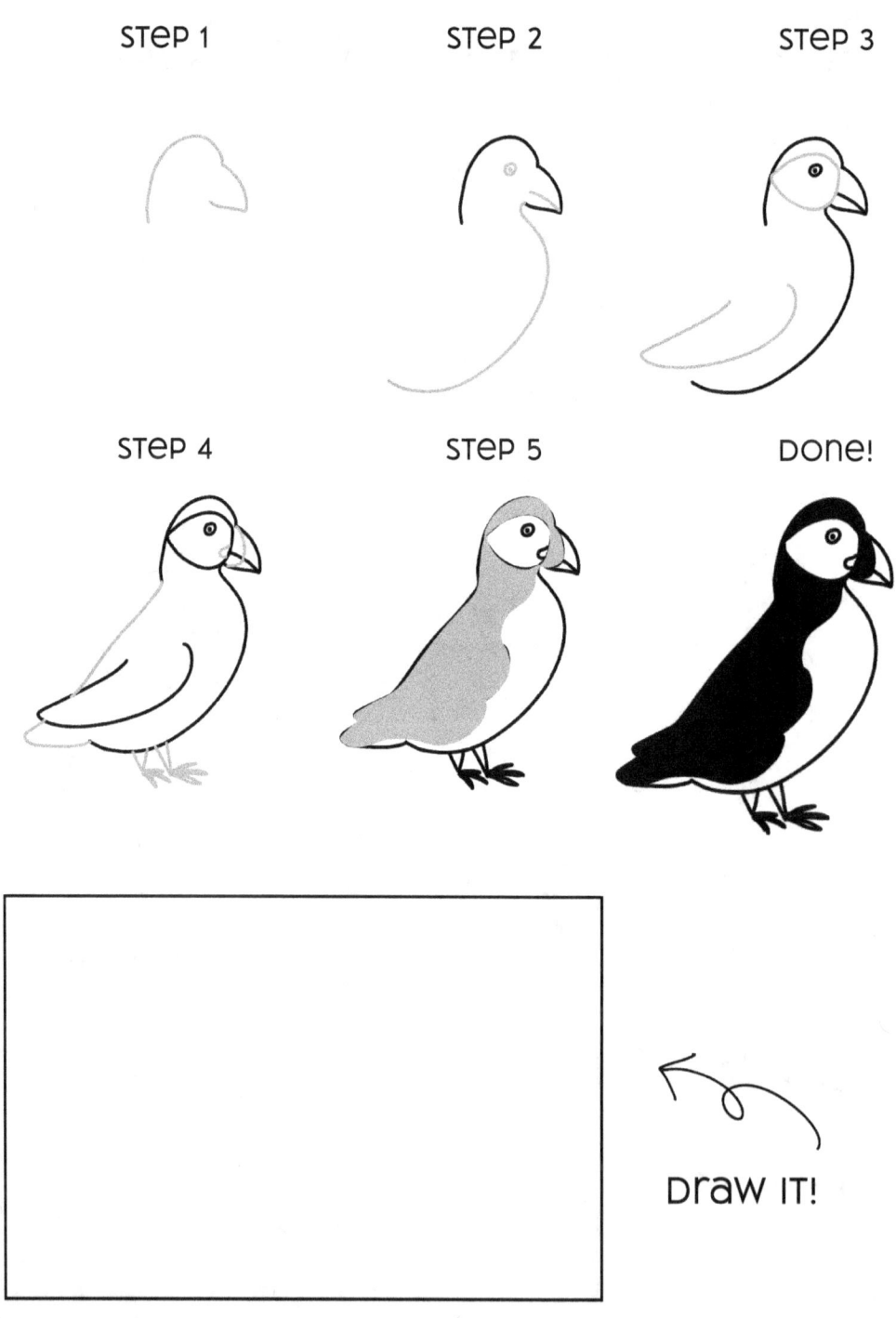

DRAW IT!

　COAST

# penguin

STEP 1          STEP 2          STEP 3

STEP 4          STEP 5          Done!

Draw IT!

# PIGEON

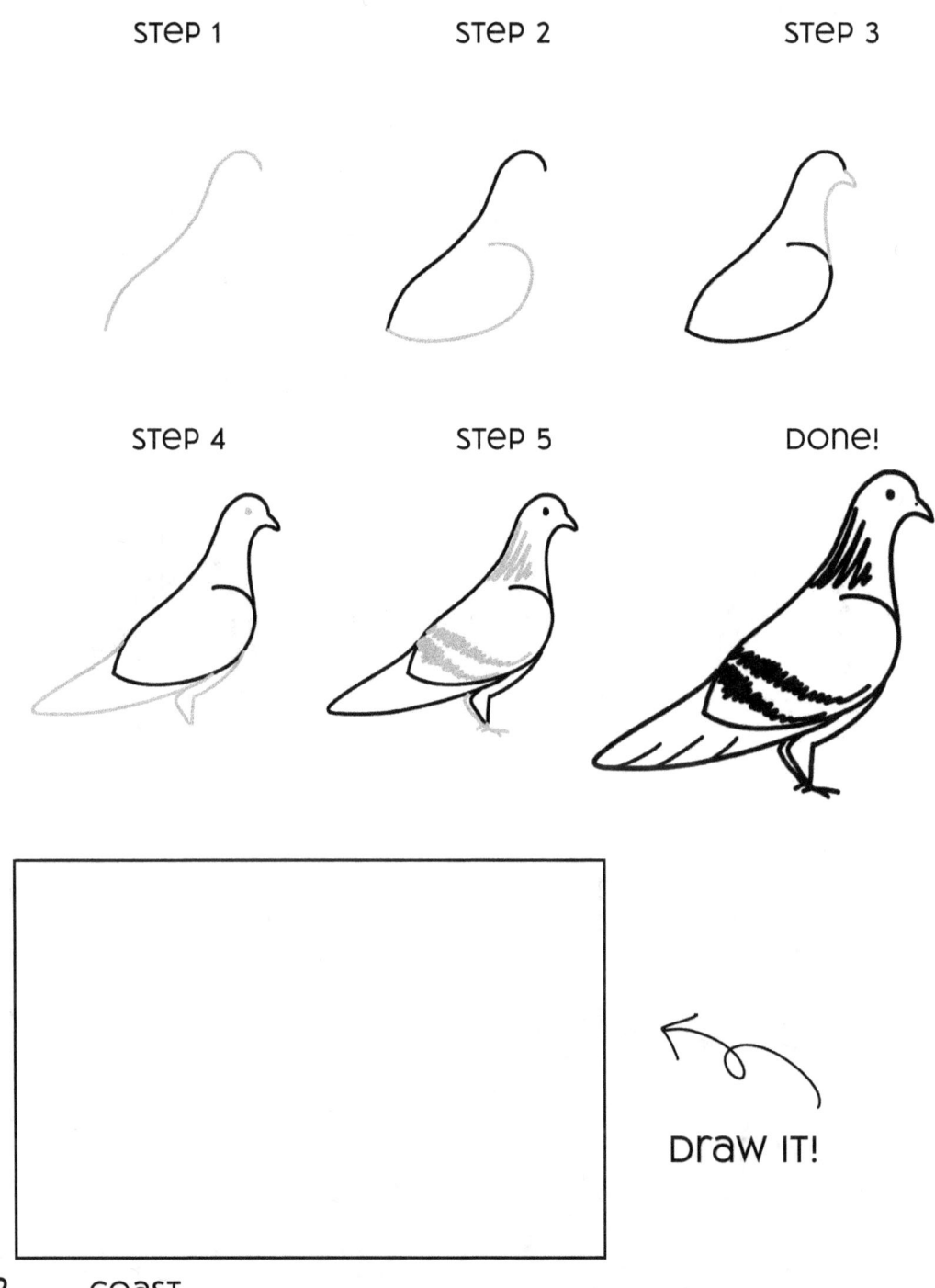

STEP 1　　STEP 2　　STEP 3

STEP 4　　STEP 5　　Done!

Draw it!

　COAST

# pelican

STEP 1

STEP 2

STEP 3

STEP 4

STEP 5

Done!

Draw it!

coast    83

underwater

# OCTOPUS

STEP 1

STEP 2

STEP 3

STEP 4

STEP 5

Done!

DRAW IT!

underwater

# SQUID

STEP 1

STEP 2

STEP 3

STEP 4

STEP 5

Done!

DRAW IT!

# orca

STEP 1

STEP 2

STEP 3

STEP 4

STEP 5

Done!

DRAW IT!

underwater

# HUMPBACK WHALE

STEP 1

STEP 2

STEP 3

STEP 4

STEP 5

Done!

Draw it!

# shark

STEP 1             STEP 2             STEP 3

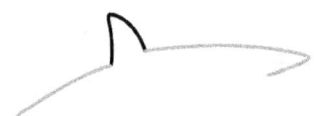 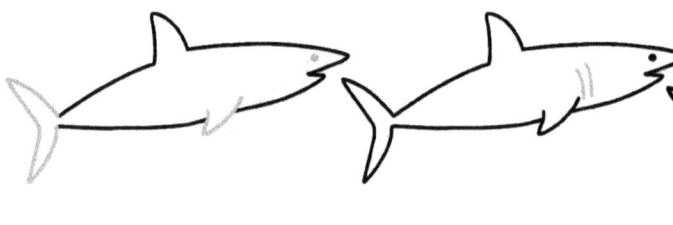

STEP 4             STEP 5             Done!

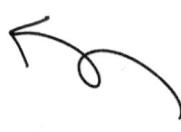

Draw it!

90      underwater

# DOLPHIN

STEP 1  STEP 2  STEP 3

STEP 4  STEP 5  Done!

Draw it!

# narwhal

STEP 1

STEP 2

STEP 3

STEP 4

STEP 5

Done!

DRAW IT!

underwater

# manatee

STEP 1

STEP 2

STEP 3

STEP 4

STEP 5

DONE!

Draw it!

# STINGRAY

STEP 1                    STEP 2                    STEP 3

STEP 4                    STEP 5                    Done!

Draw It!

underwater

# sea turtle

STEP 1

STEP 2

STEP 3

STEP 4

STEP 5

DONE!

DRAW IT!

# CRAB

STEP 1

STEP 2

STEP 3

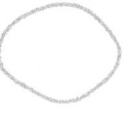
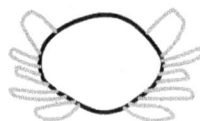

STEP 4

STEP 5

DONE!

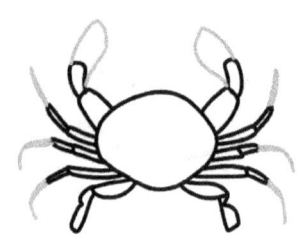
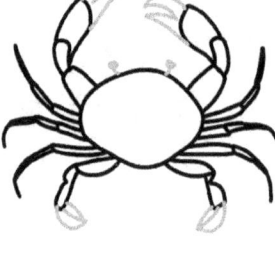
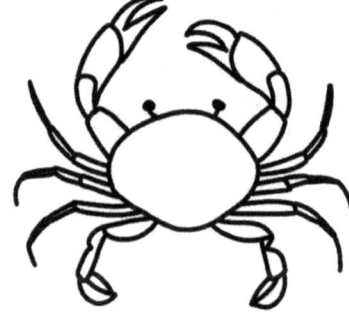

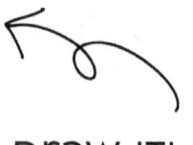

DRAW IT!

# LOBSTER

STEP 1

STEP 2

STEP 3

STEP 4

STEP 5

DONE!

DRAW IT!

# seaHorse

STEP 1            STEP 2            STEP 3

STEP 4            STEP 5            Done!

Draw It!

underwater

# seal

STEP 1    STEP 2    STEP 3

STEP 4    STEP 5    Done!

Draw it!

# clam

STEP 1

STEP 2

STEP 3

STEP 4

STEP 5

Done!

DRAW IT!

# starfish

STEP 1                    STEP 2                    STEP 3

STEP 4                    STEP 5                    Done!

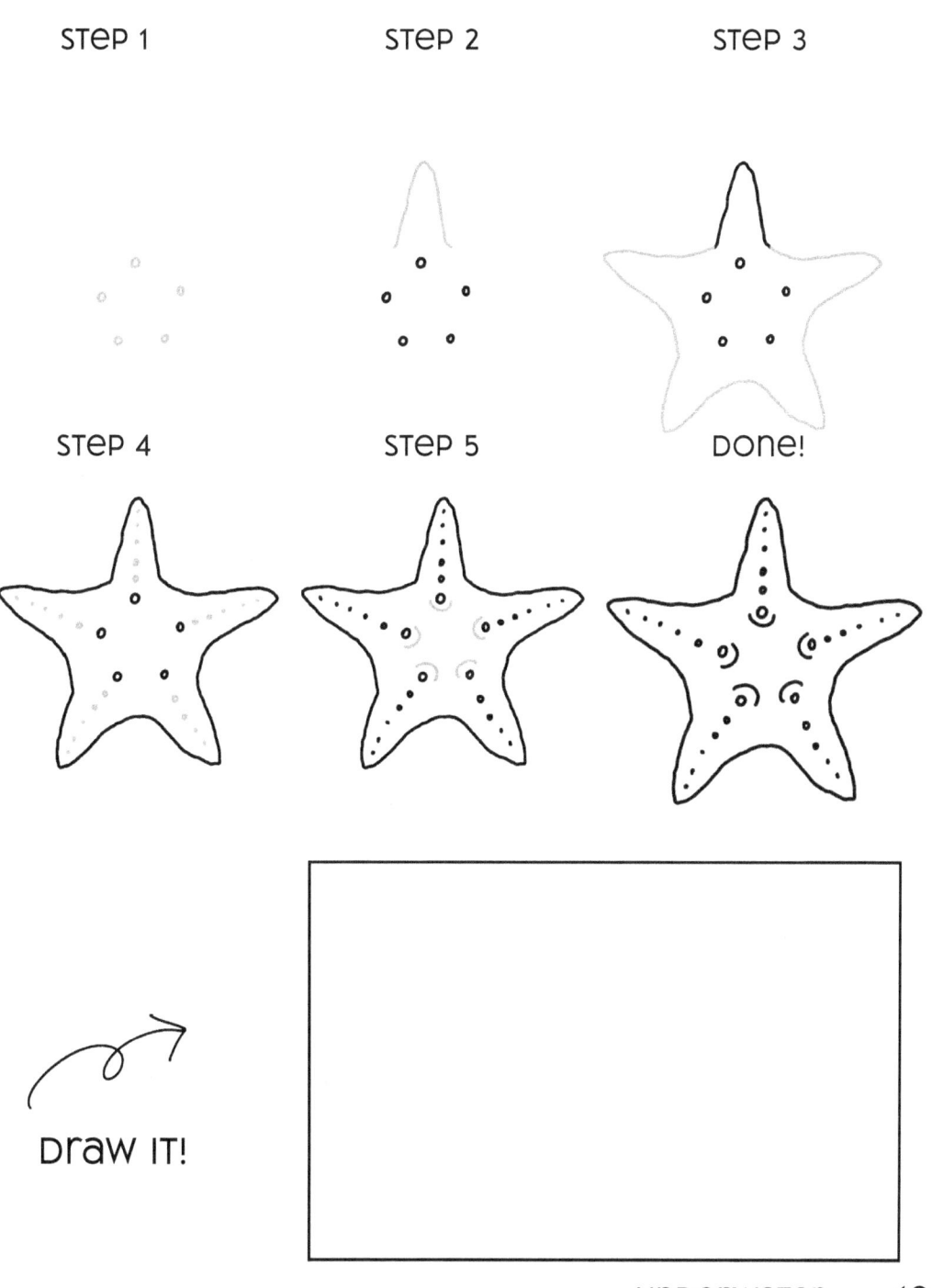

Draw it!

# JELLYFISH

STEP 1                    STEP 2                    STEP 3

STEP 4                    STEP 5                    Done!

Draw it!

underwater

# SWOrDFISH

STEP 1

STEP 2

STEP 3

STEP 4

STEP 5

Done!

Draw IT!

# CLOWNFISH

### STEP 1
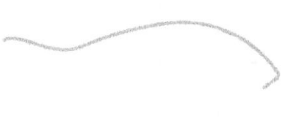

### STEP 2
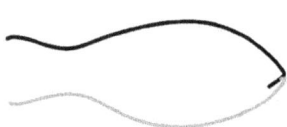

### STEP 3
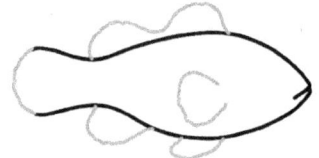

### STEP 4
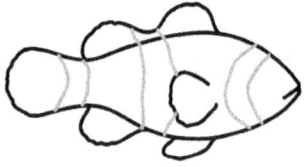

### STEP 5
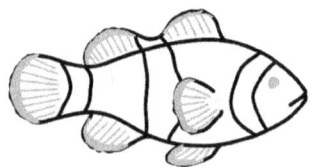

### Done!
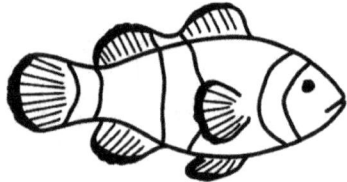

Draw IT!

# PUFFErFISH

STEP 1 STEP 2 STEP 3

STEP 4 STEP 5 DONE!

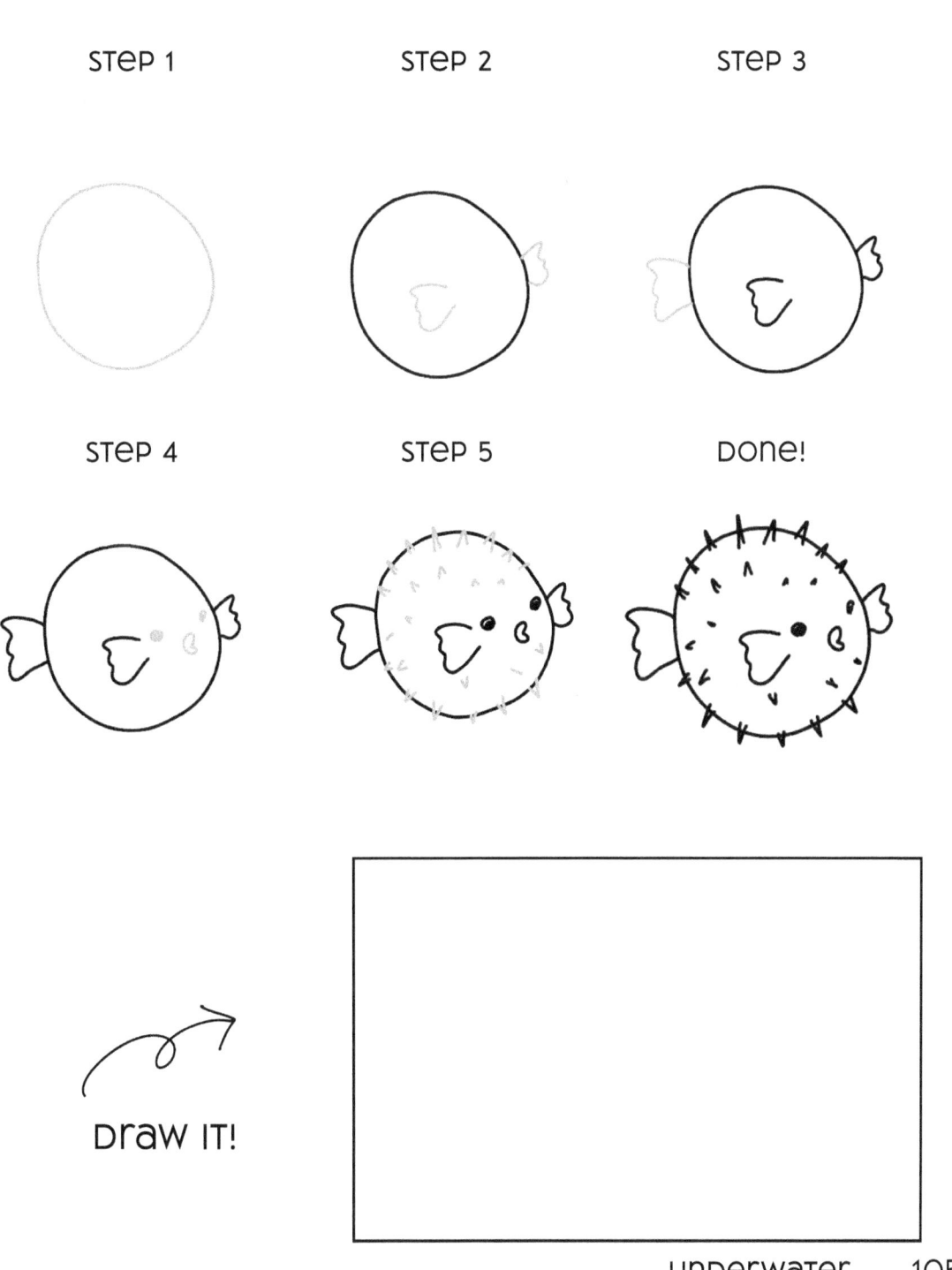

DRAW IT!

# HaDDOCK

STEP 1

STEP 2

STEP 3

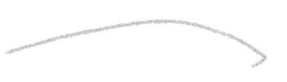 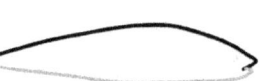 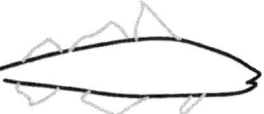

STEP 4

STEP 5

DONE!

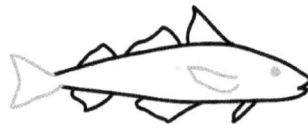 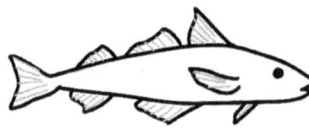 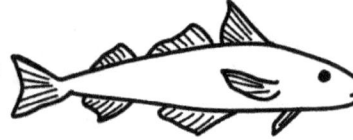

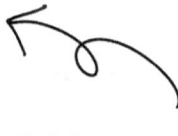

Draw IT!

underwater

# angelfish

STEP 1

STEP 2

STEP 3

STEP 4

STEP 5

Done!

Draw IT!

# HALIBUT

STEP 1     STEP 2     STEP 3

STEP 4     STEP 5     DONE!

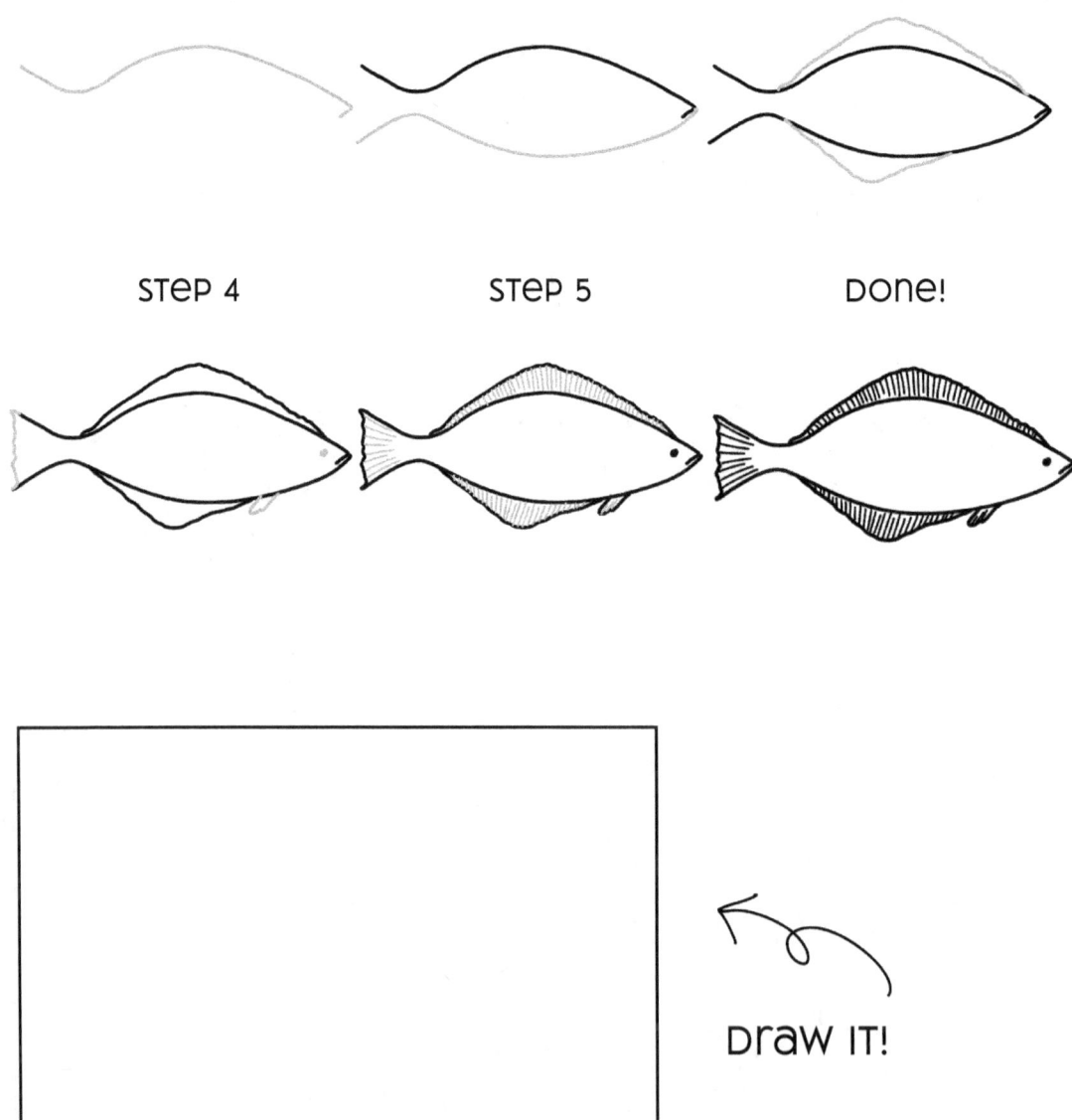

DRAW IT!

underwater

next up... jungle & rainforest

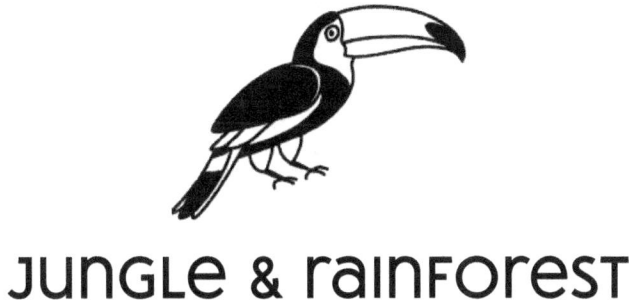

JUNGLE & RAINFOREST

# toucan

STEP 1

STEP 2

STEP 3

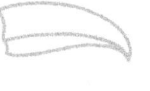

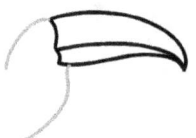

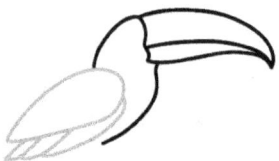

STEP 4

STEP 5

Done!

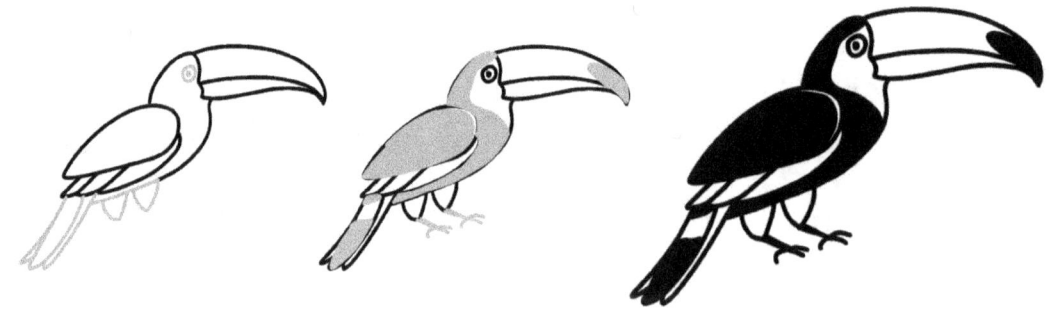

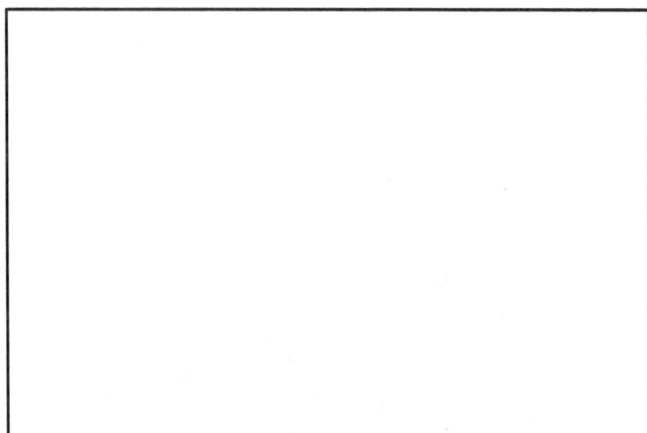

DRAW IT!

JUNGLE & RAINFOREST

# macaw

STEP 1          STEP 2          STEP 3

STEP 4          STEP 5          Done!

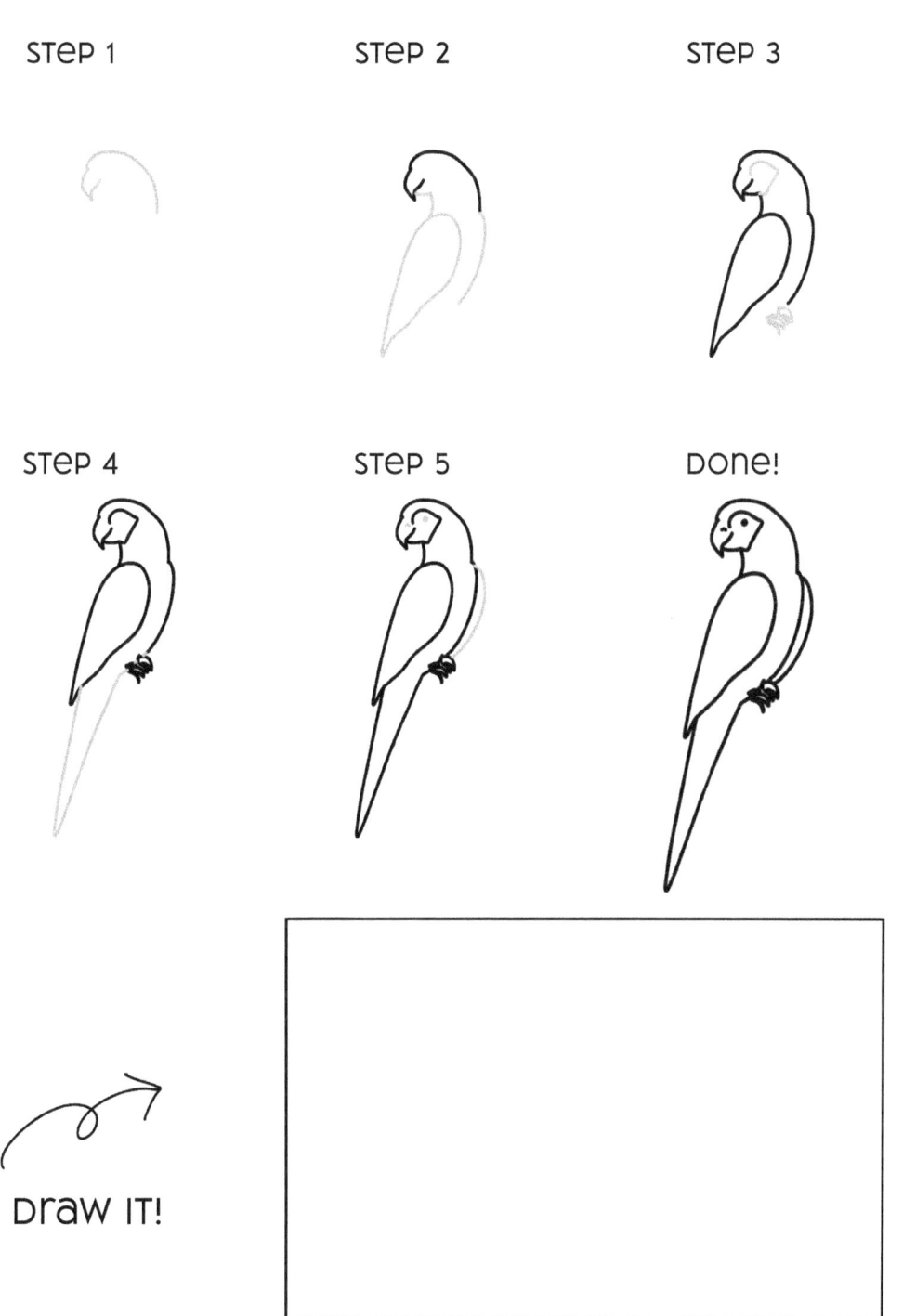

Draw it!

# KOOKABURRA

STEP 1            STEP 2            STEP 3

STEP 4            STEP 5            DONE!

DRAW IT!

# BAT

STEP 1

STEP 2

STEP 3

STEP 4

STEP 5

DONE!

DRAW IT!

# CHaMeLeon

STEP 1          STEP 2          STEP 3

STEP 4          STEP 5          Done!

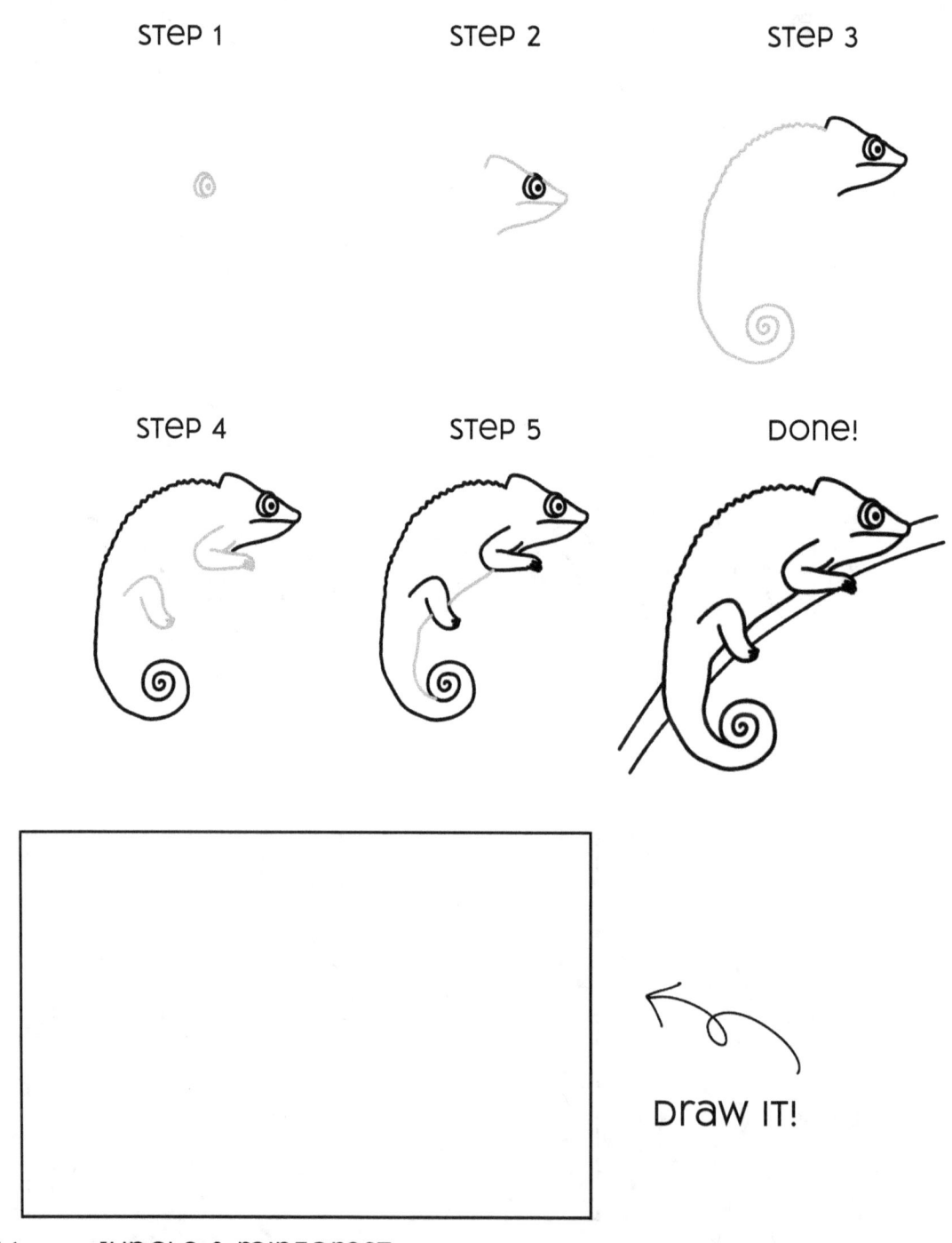

DRAW IT!

JUNGLE & rainForest

# Gecko

STEP 1    STEP 2    STEP 3

STEP 4    STEP 5    Done!

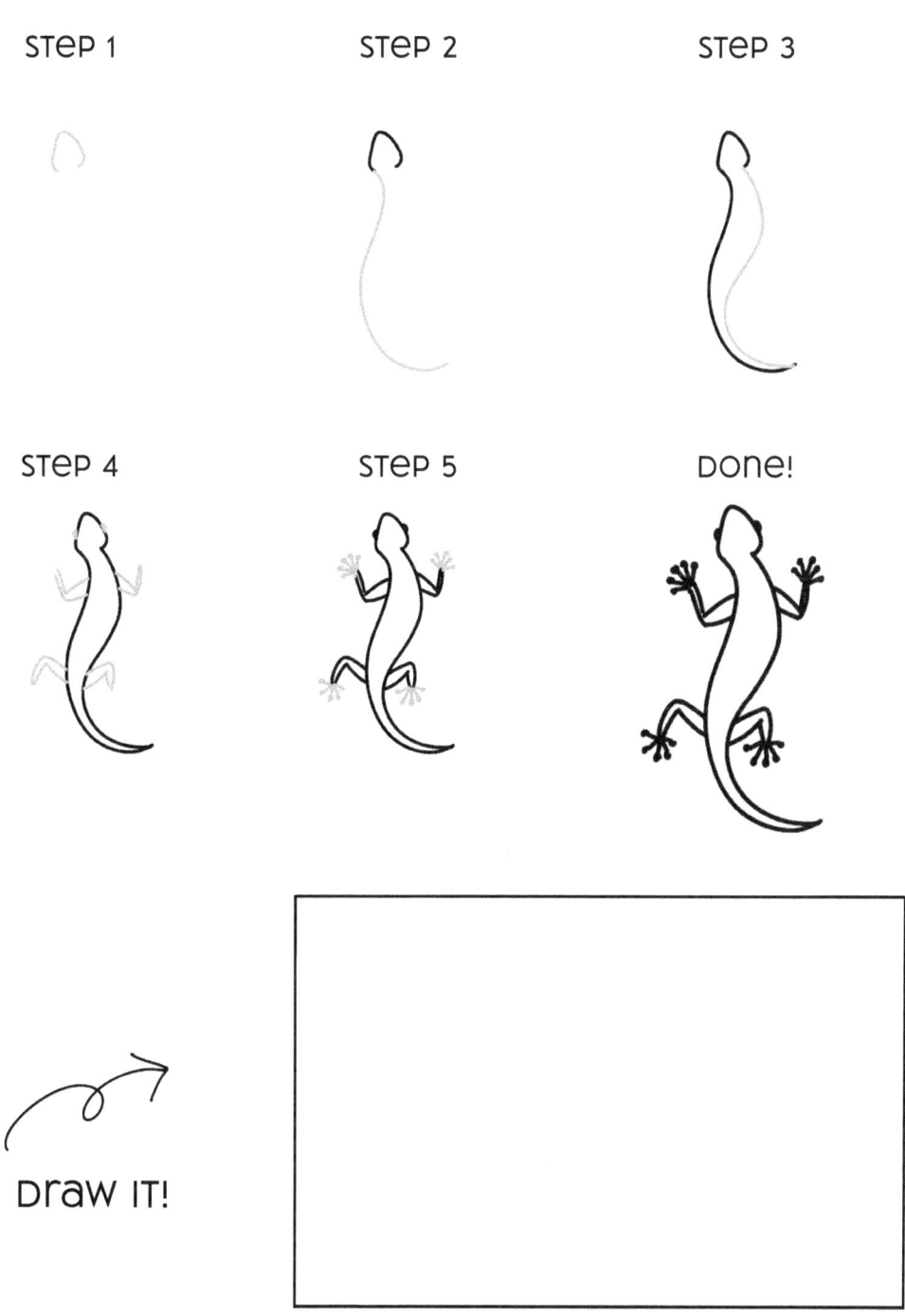

Draw it!

# SLOTH

STEP 1          STEP 2          STEP 3

STEP 4          STEP 5          DONE!

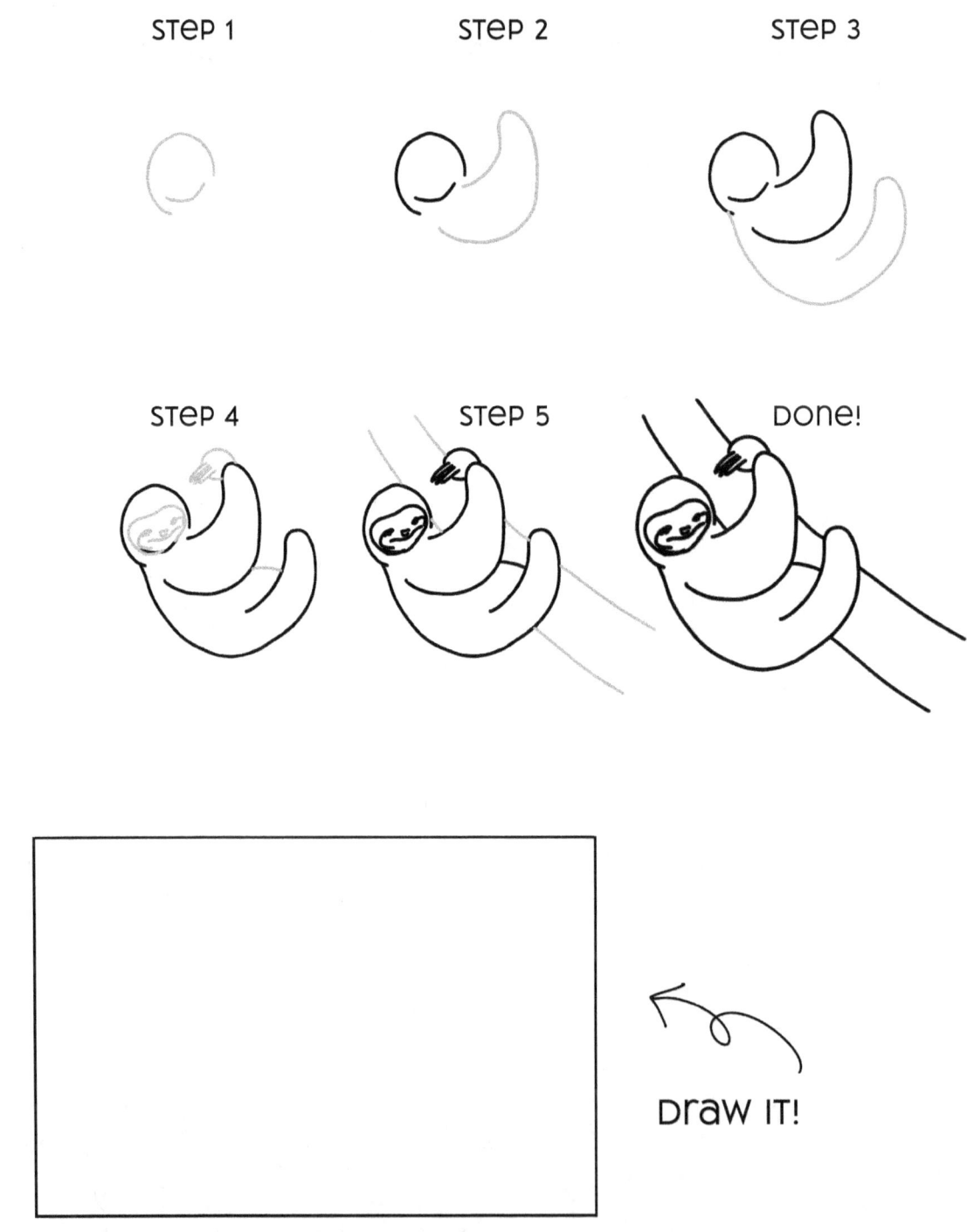

DRAW IT!

# Lemur

STEP 1  STEP 2  STEP 3

STEP 4  STEP 5  DONE!

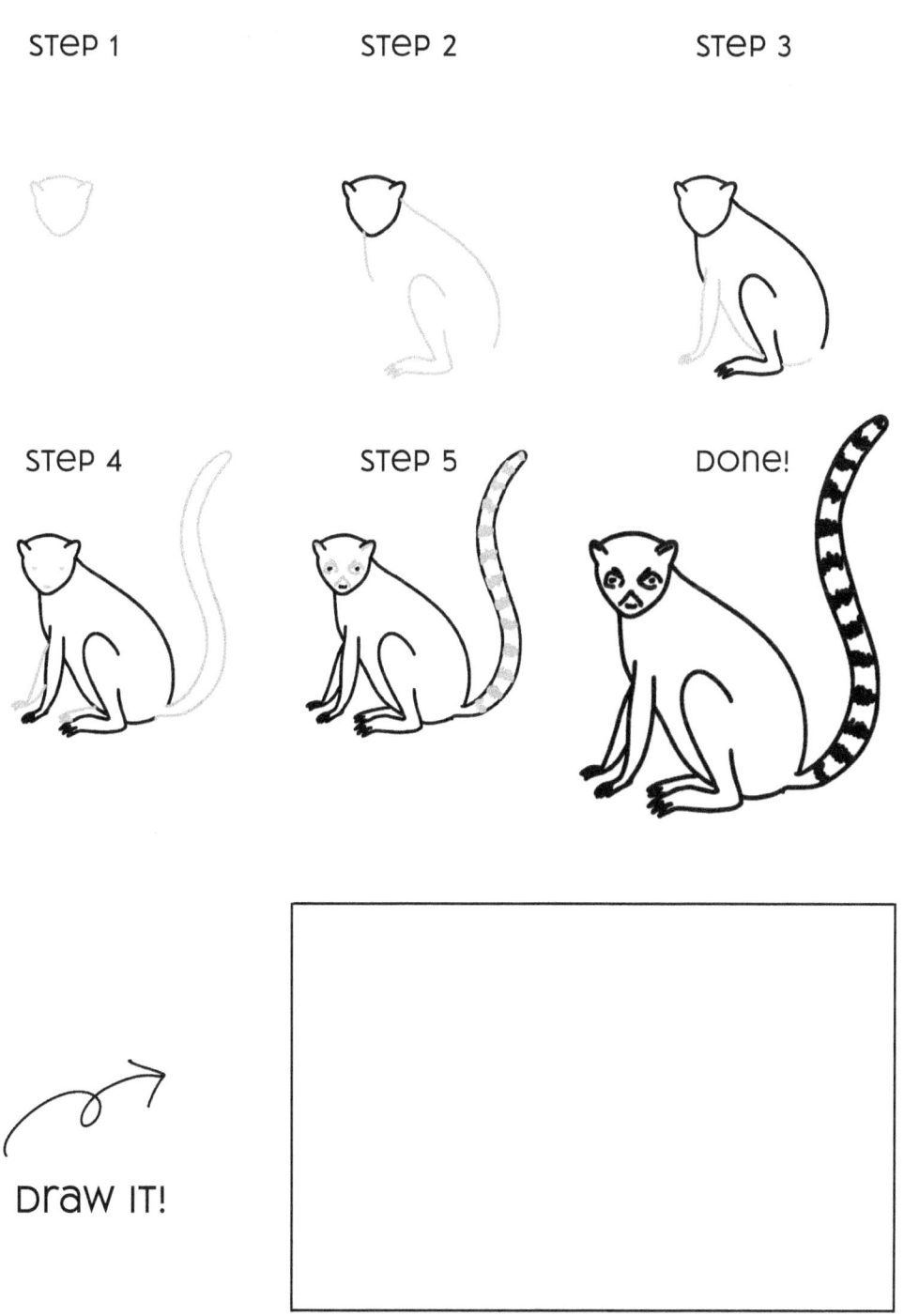

DRAW IT!

# panda

STEP 1         STEP 2         STEP 3

STEP 4         STEP 5         Done!

DRAW IT!

Jungle & rainforest

# Tiger

STEP 1

STEP 2

STEP 3

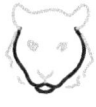

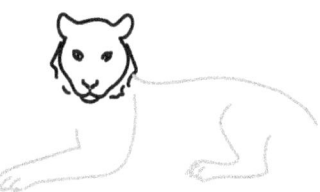

STEP 4

STEP 5

DONE!

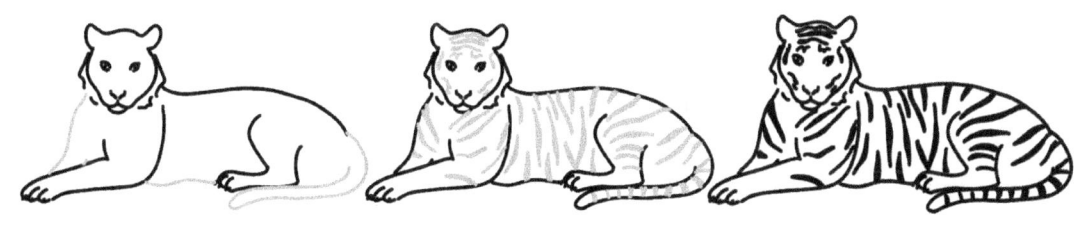

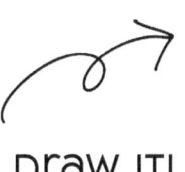

DRAW IT!

# Gorilla

STEP 1

STEP 2

STEP 3

STEP 4

STEP 5

Done!

Draw it!

Jungle & rainforest

# marmoset

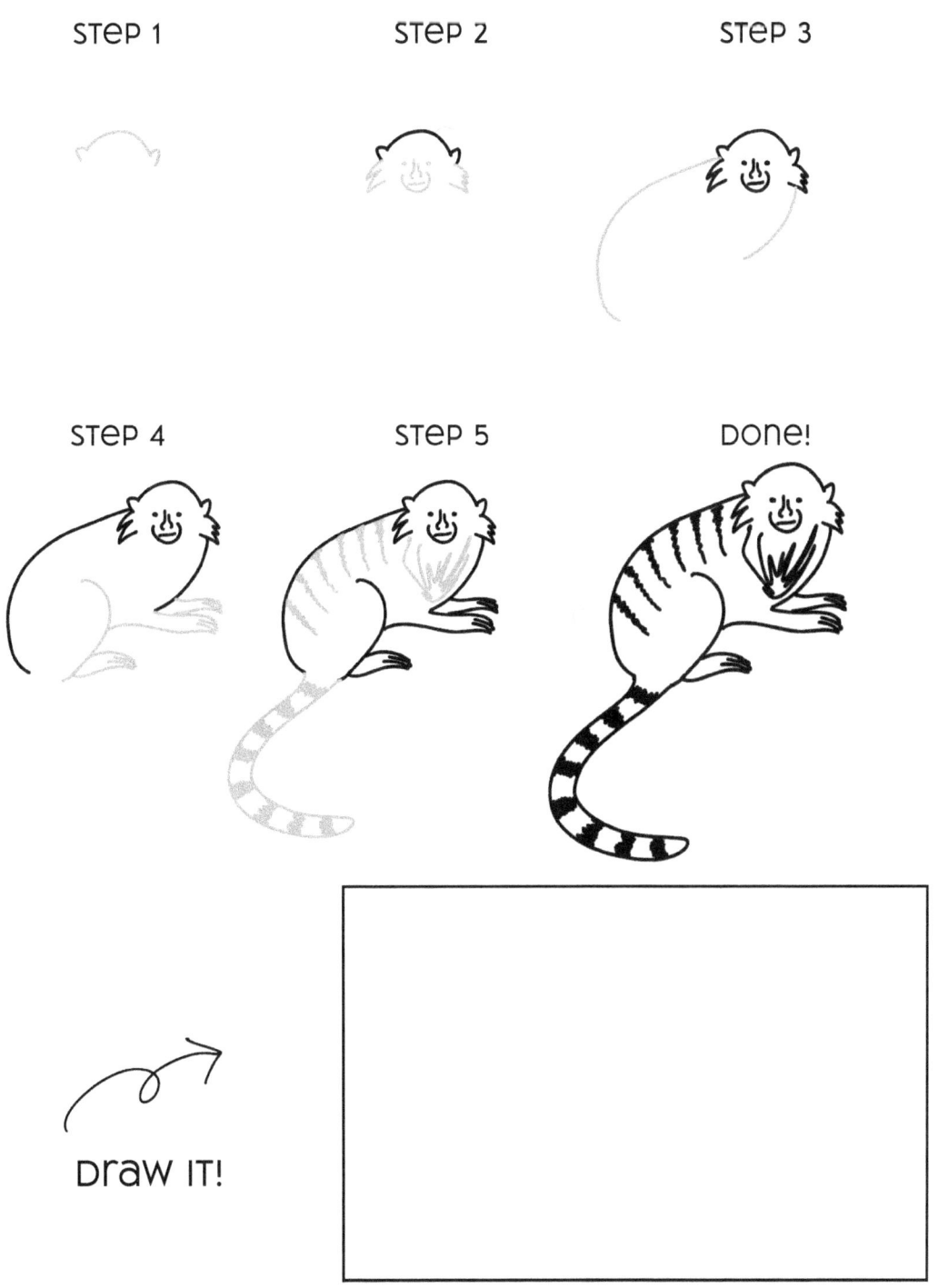

STEP 1

STEP 2

STEP 3

STEP 4

STEP 5

Done!

Draw it!

# macaque

STEP 1  STEP 2  STEP 3

STEP 4  STEP 5  Done!

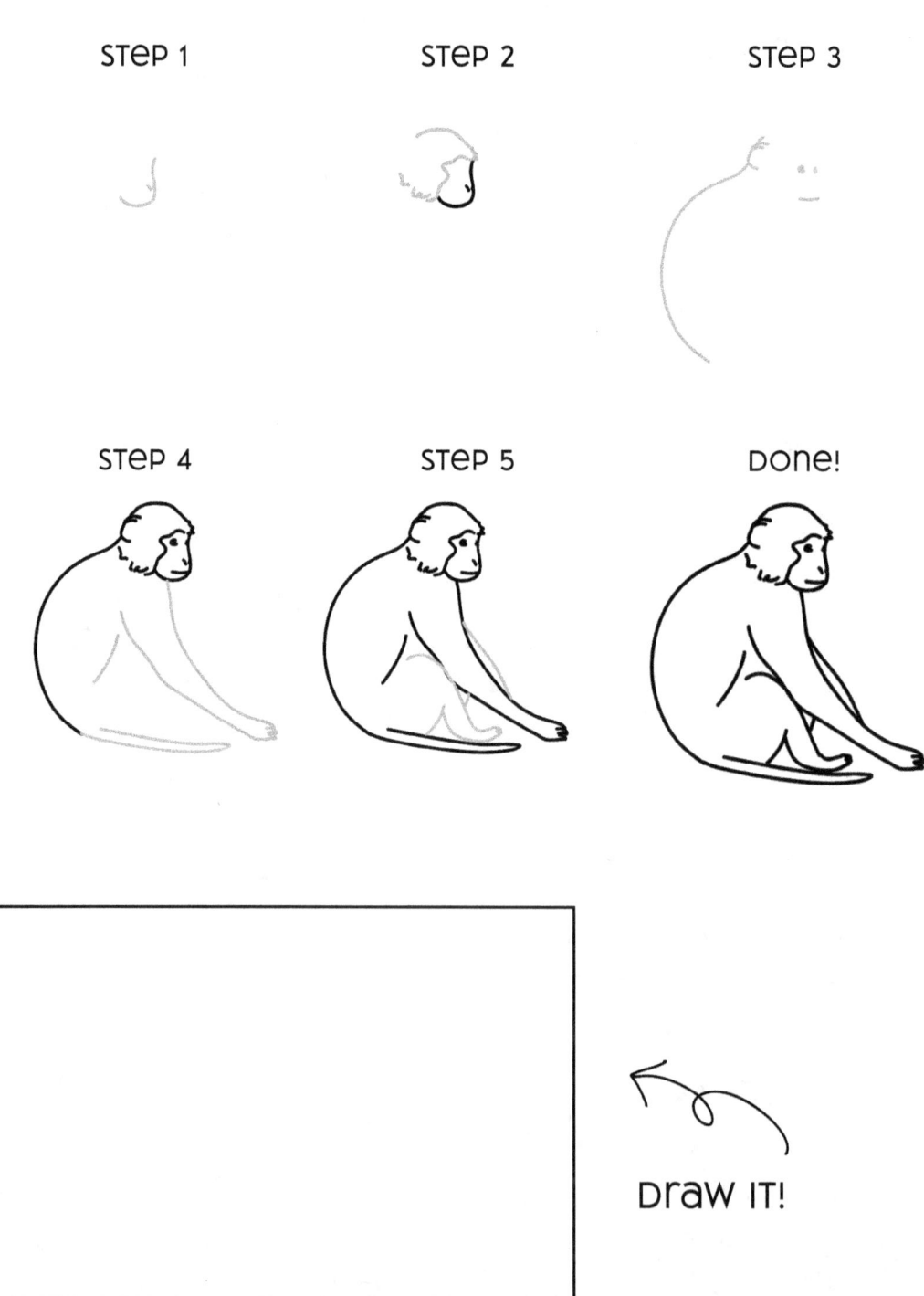

Draw It!

next up... savanna

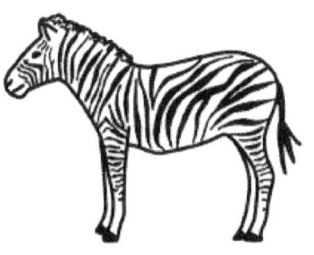

savanna

# BADGER

STEP 1        STEP 2        STEP 3

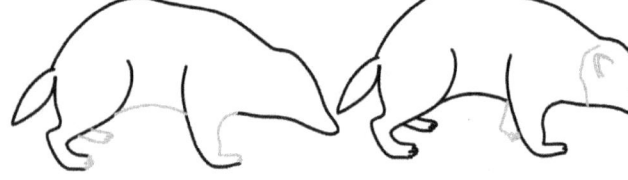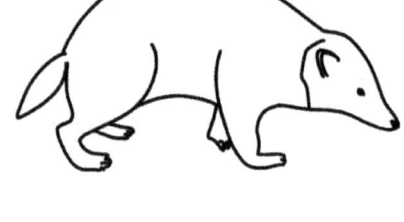

STEP 4        STEP 5        Done!

DRAW IT!

   savanna

# aardvark

STEP 1

STEP 2

STEP 3

STEP 4

STEP 5

Done!

Draw it!

savanna     129

# Giraffe

STEP 1

STEP 2

STEP 3

STEP 4

STEP 5

Done!

DRAW IT!

savanna

# zeBra

STEP 1             STEP 2             STEP 3

STEP 4             STEP 5             Done!

Draw IT!

# LION

STEP 1     STEP 2     STEP 3

STEP 4     STEP 5     DONE!

DRAW IT!

savanna

# cheetah

STEP 1　　　　STEP 2　　　　STEP 3

STEP 4　　　　STEP 5　　　　Done!

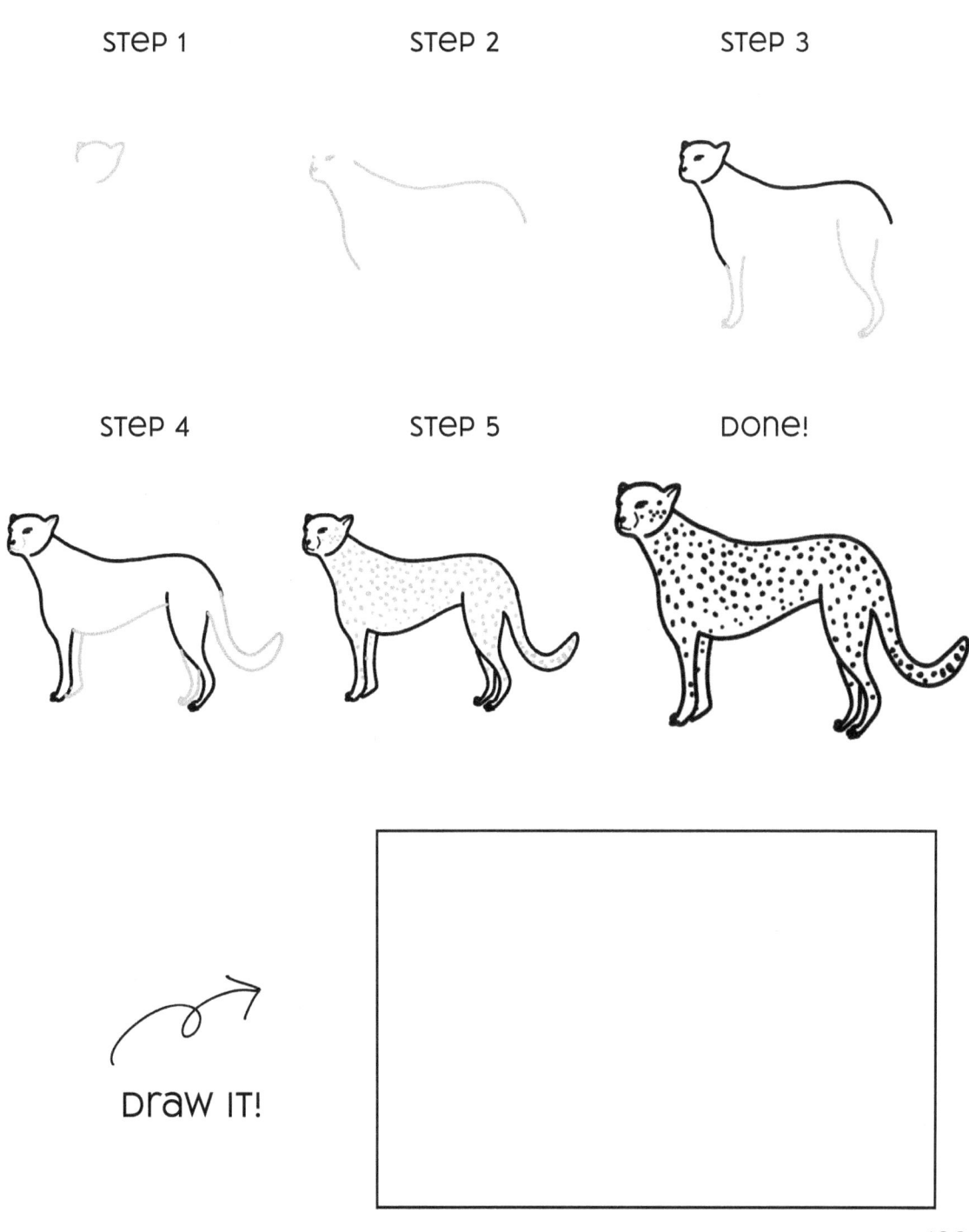

Draw it!

# rHINoceros

STEP 1

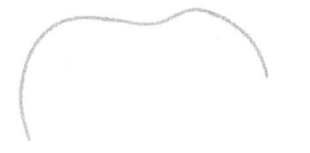

STEP 2

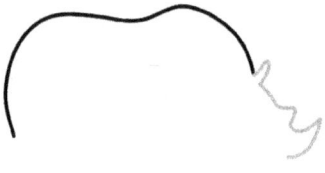

STEP 3

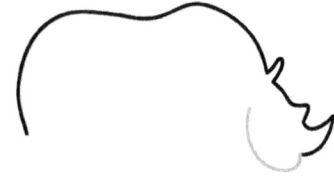

STEP 4

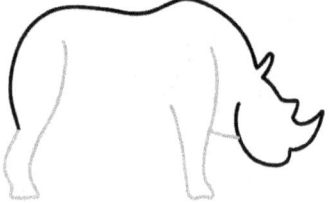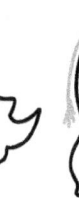

STEP 5

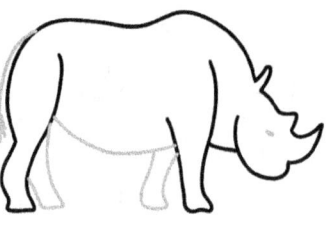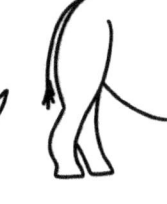

Done!

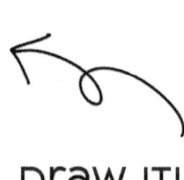

DRAW IT!

savanna

# elephant

STEP 1       STEP 2       STEP 3

STEP 4       STEP 5       DONE!

Draw IT!

savanna    135

# KOMODO DRAGON

STEP 1

STEP 2

STEP 3

STEP 4

STEP 5

DONE!

DRAW IT!

savanna

# warthog

STEP 1

STEP 2

STEP 3

STEP 4

STEP 5

Done!

Draw it!

# kangaroo

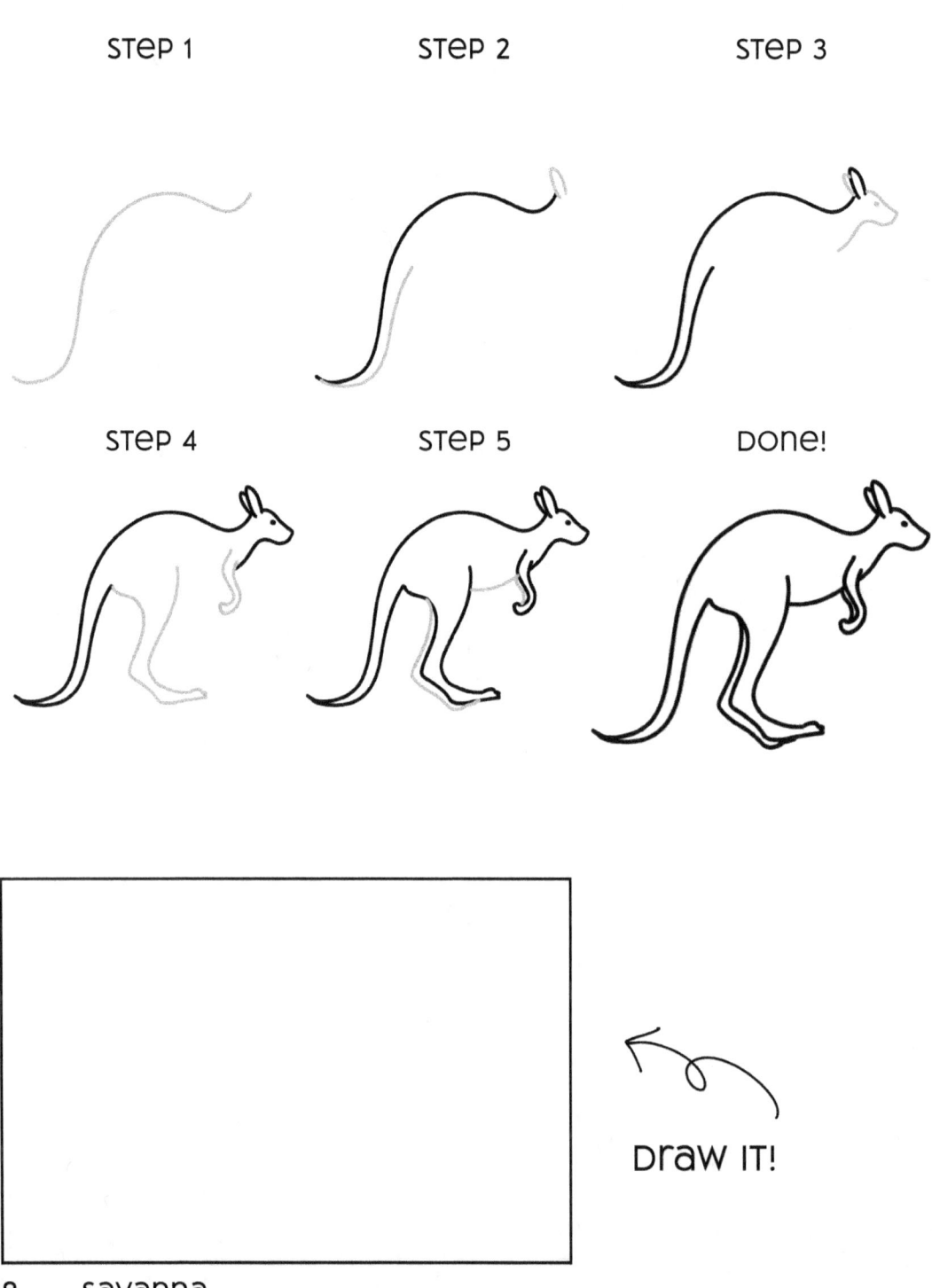

STEP 1      STEP 2      STEP 3

STEP 4      STEP 5      Done!

Draw IT!

savanna

# DIK DIK

STEP 1          STEP 2          STEP 3

STEP 4          STEP 5          Done!

Draw it!

# antelope

STEP 1

STEP 2

STEP 3

STEP 4

STEP 5

Done!

Draw it!

savanna

# BaBOON

STEP 1  STEP 2  STEP 3

STEP 4  STEP 5  Done!

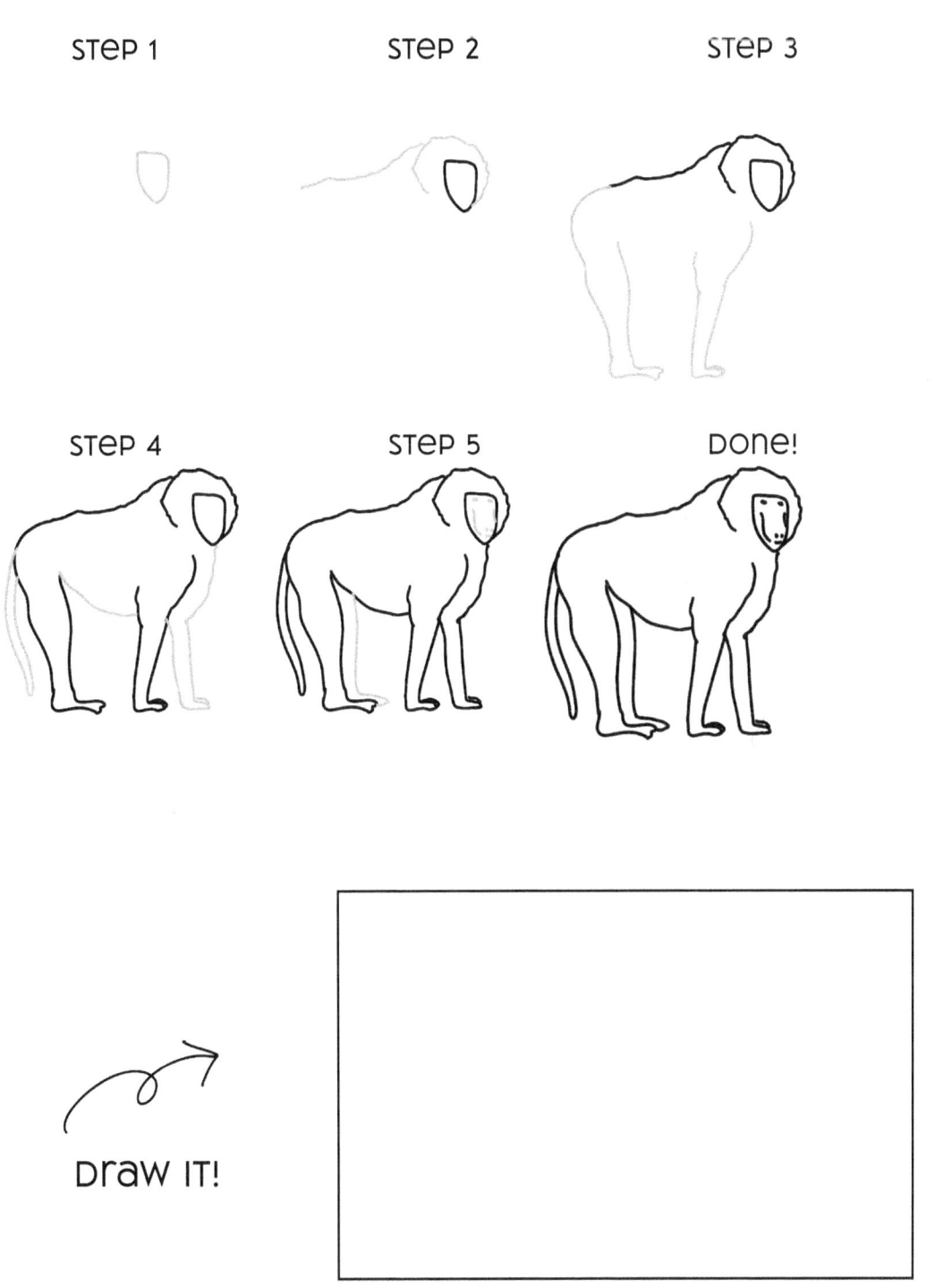

Draw IT!

# crane

STEP 1    STEP 2    STEP 3

STEP 4    STEP 5    Done!

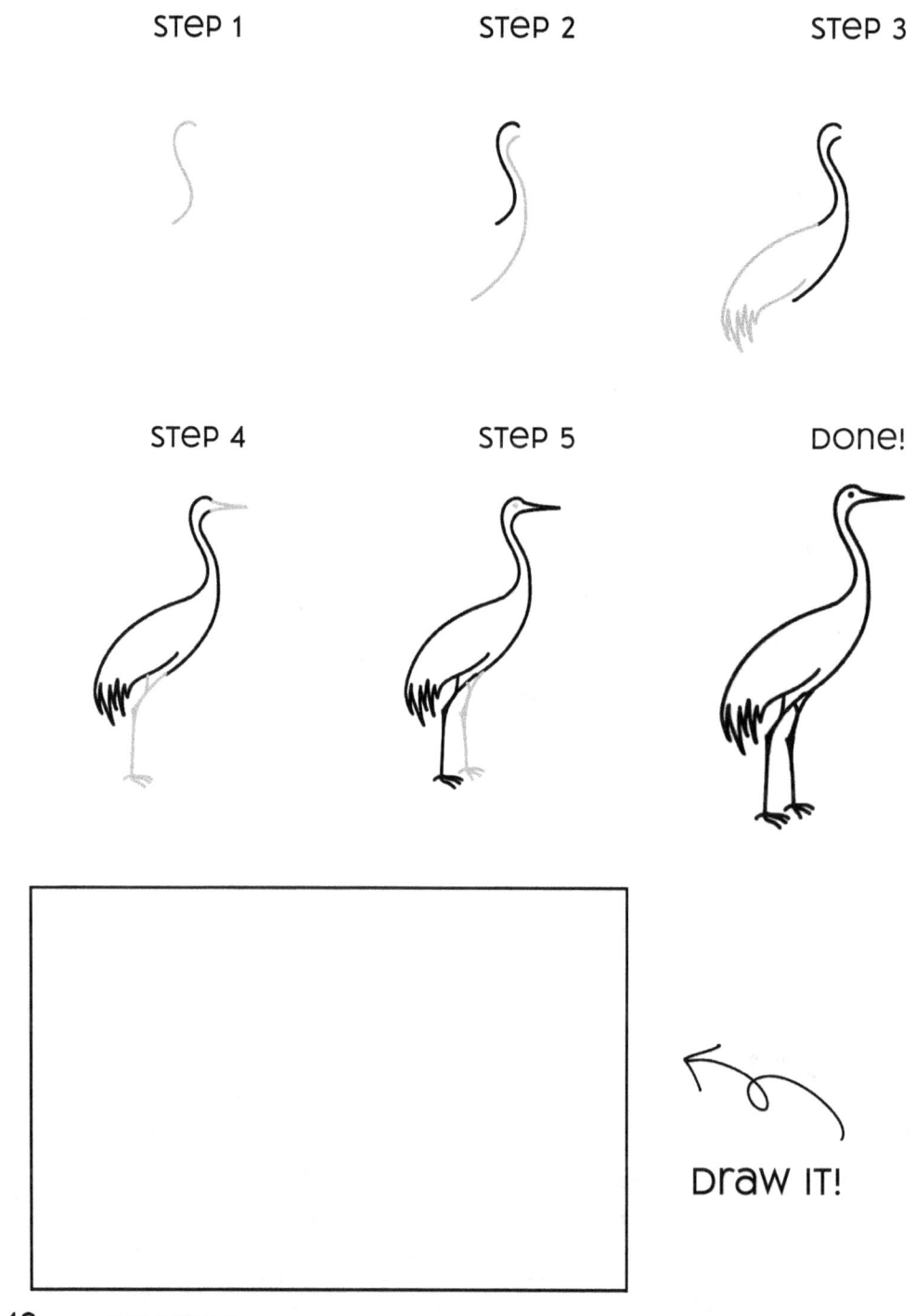

DRAW IT!

savanna

# OSTRICH

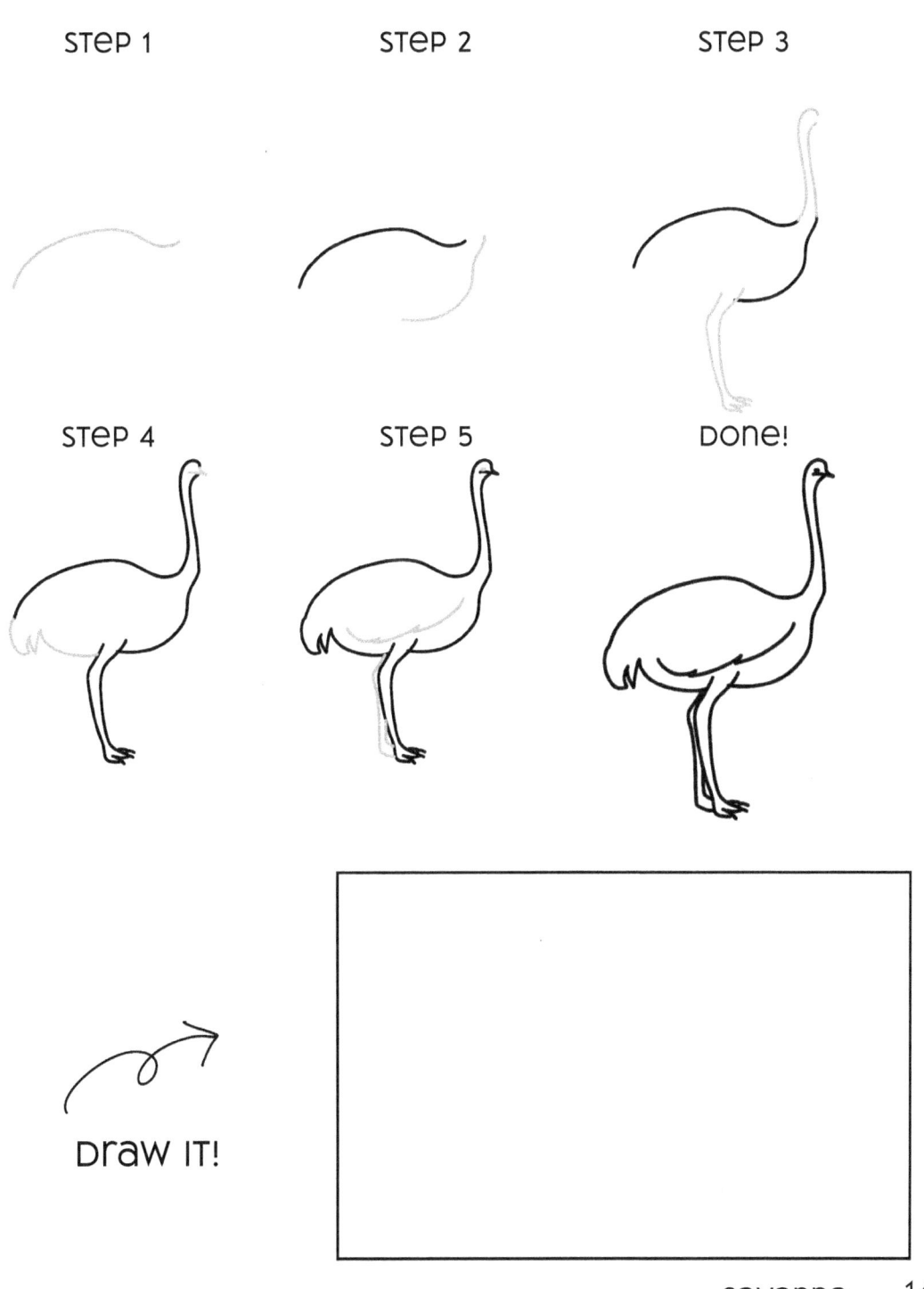

STEP 1

STEP 2

STEP 3

STEP 4

STEP 5

Done!

Draw it!

# COCKATIEL

STEP 1

STEP 2

STEP 3

STEP 4

STEP 5

DONE!

DRAW IT!

savanna

next up... desert

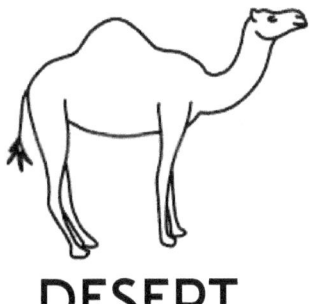

DESERT

# camel

STEP 1

STEP 2

STEP 3

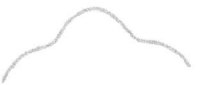 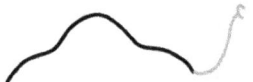 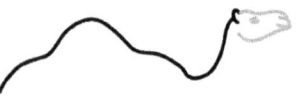

STEP 4

STEP 5

Done!

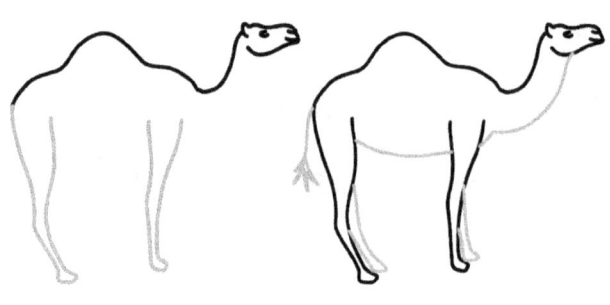 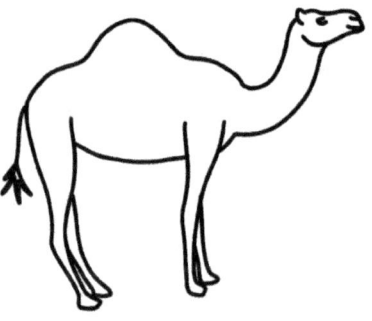 

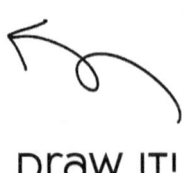

Draw IT!

Desert

# rattlesnake

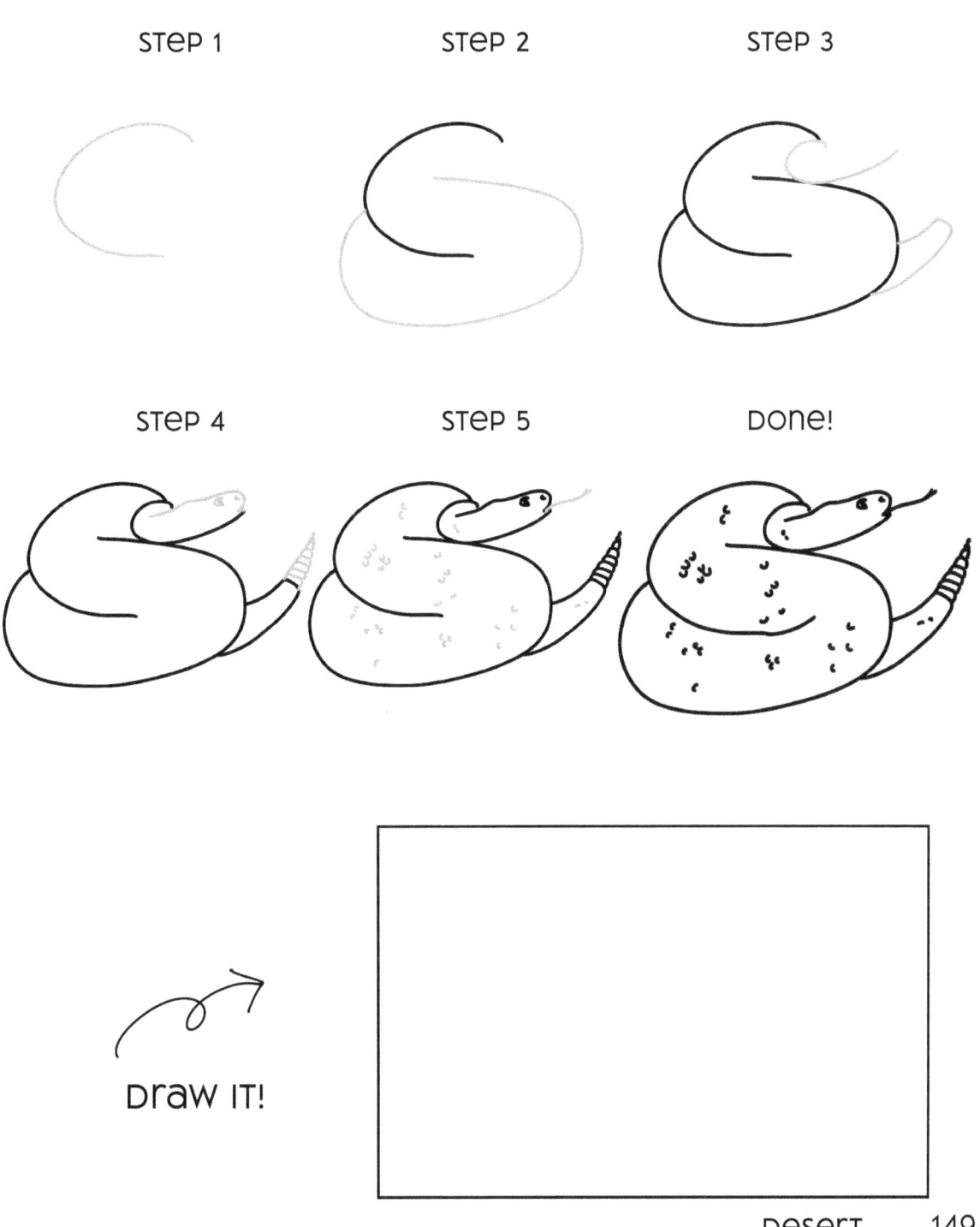

STEP 1  STEP 2  STEP 3

STEP 4  STEP 5  Done!

Draw it!

# DONKEY

STEP 1

STEP 2

STEP 3

STEP 4

STEP 5

Done!

Draw IT!

Desert

# mule

STEP 1

STEP 2

STEP 3

STEP 4

STEP 5

Done!

Draw It!

# BURROWING OWL

STEP 1

STEP 2

STEP 3

STEP 4

STEP 5

Done!

Draw It!

desert

# roaprunner

STEP 1              STEP 2              STEP 3

STEP 4              STEP 5              Done!

Draw IT!

# Hamster

STEP 1

STEP 2

STEP 3

STEP 4

STEP 5

Done!

DRAW IT!

154    Desert

next up... insects

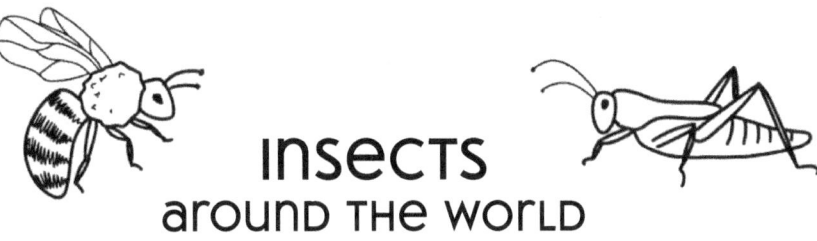

# insects
## around the world

# YELLOW JACKET

### STEP 1

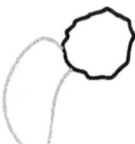

### STEP 2

### STEP 3

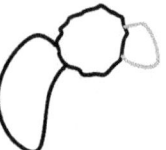

### STEP 4

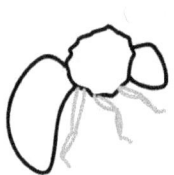

### STEP 5

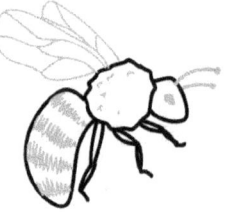

### Done!

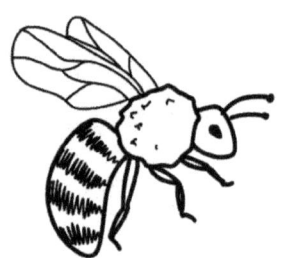

Draw IT!

insects

# BUMBLEBEE

STEP 1

STEP 2

STEP 3

STEP 4

STEP 5

DONE!

DRAW IT!

# FIREFLY

STEP 1

STEP 2

STEP 3

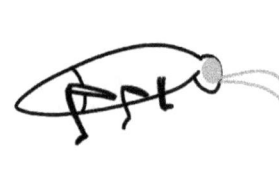

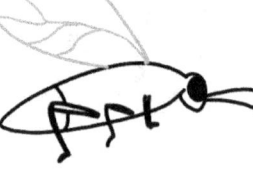

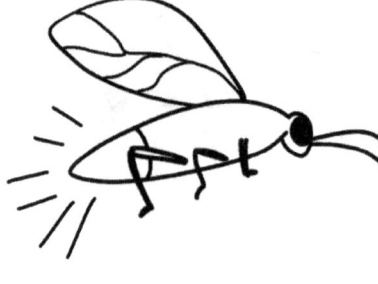

STEP 4

STEP 5

Done!

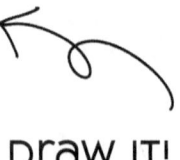

Draw IT!

# ant

STEP 1

STEP 2

STEP 3

STEP 4

STEP 5

DONE!

DRAW IT!

# PRAYING MANTIS

STEP 1

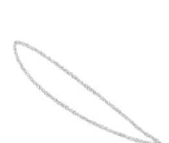

STEP 2

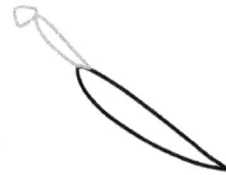

STEP 3

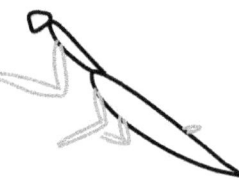

STEP 4

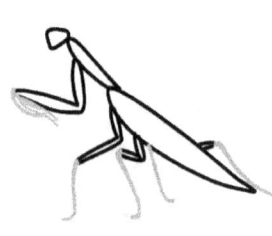

STEP 5

Done!

DRAW IT!

INSECTS

# Grasshopper

STEP 1

STEP 2

STEP 3

STEP 4

STEP 5

Done!

Draw it!

# caterpillar

STEP 1

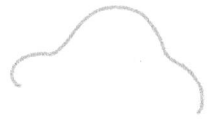

STEP 2

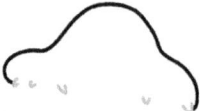

STEP 3

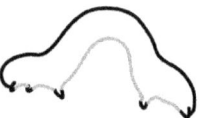

STEP 4

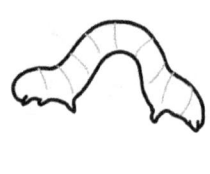

STEP 5

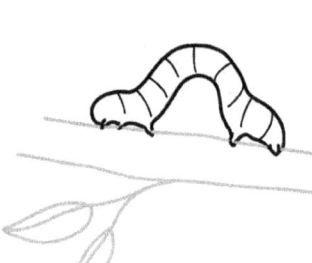

Done!

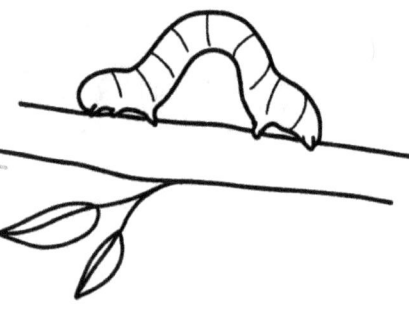

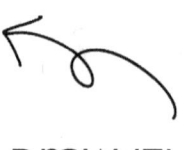

Draw IT!

INSECTS

# BUTTERFLY

STEP 1

STEP 2

STEP 3

STEP 4

STEP 5

DONE!

DRAW IT!

# MOTH

STEP 1

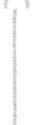

STEP 2

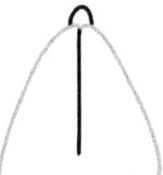

STEP 3

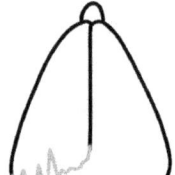

STEP 4

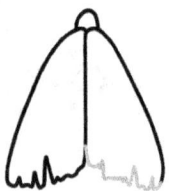

STEP 5

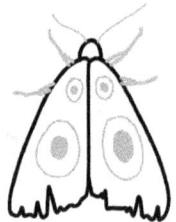

Done!

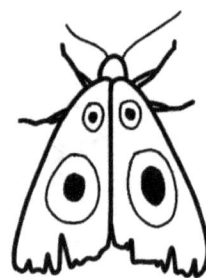

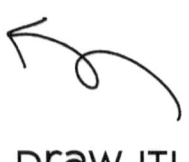

Draw it!

insects

# LADYBUG

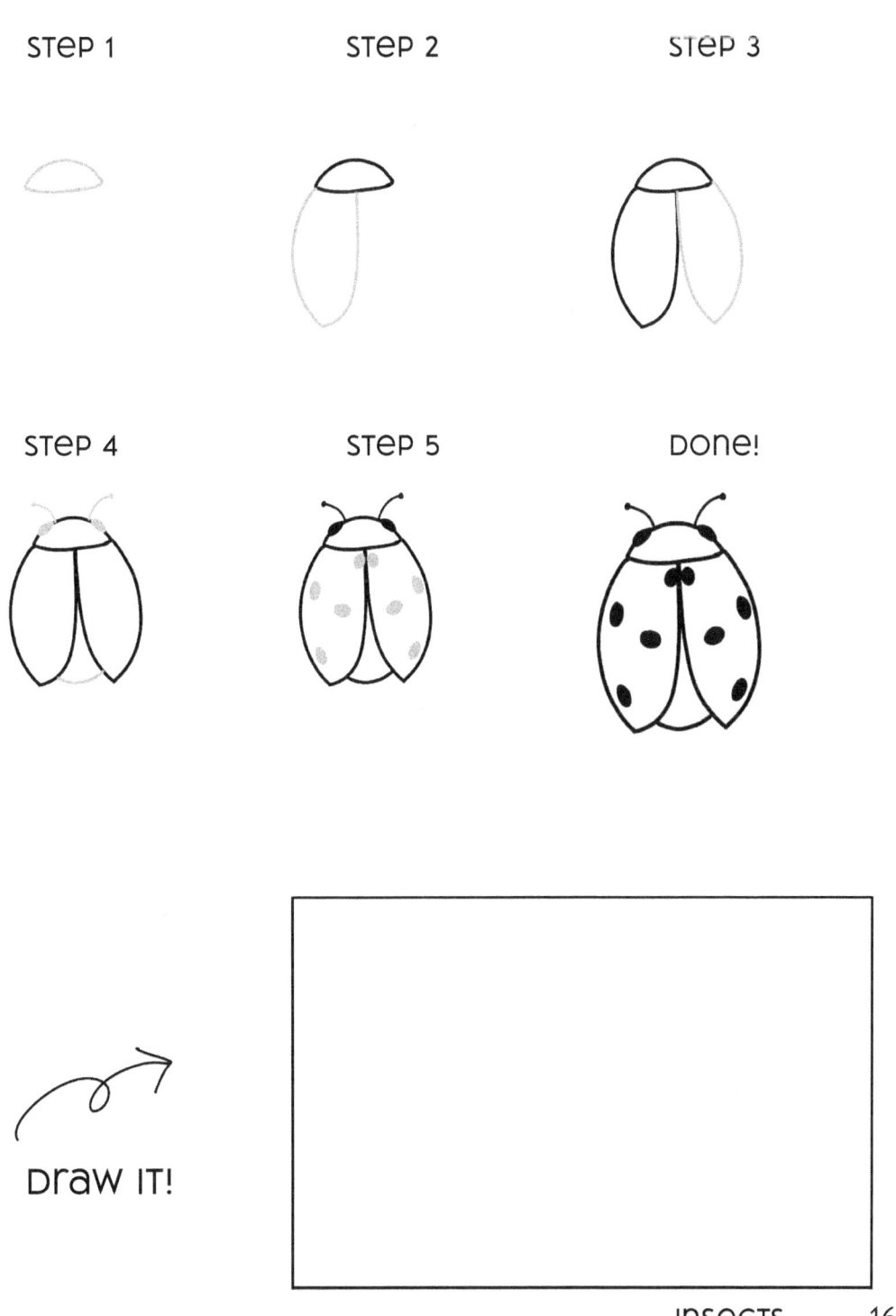

STEP 1

STEP 2

STEP 3

STEP 4

STEP 5

Done!

Draw it!

# DRAGONFLY

STEP 1          STEP 2          STEP 3

STEP 4          STEP 5          DONE!

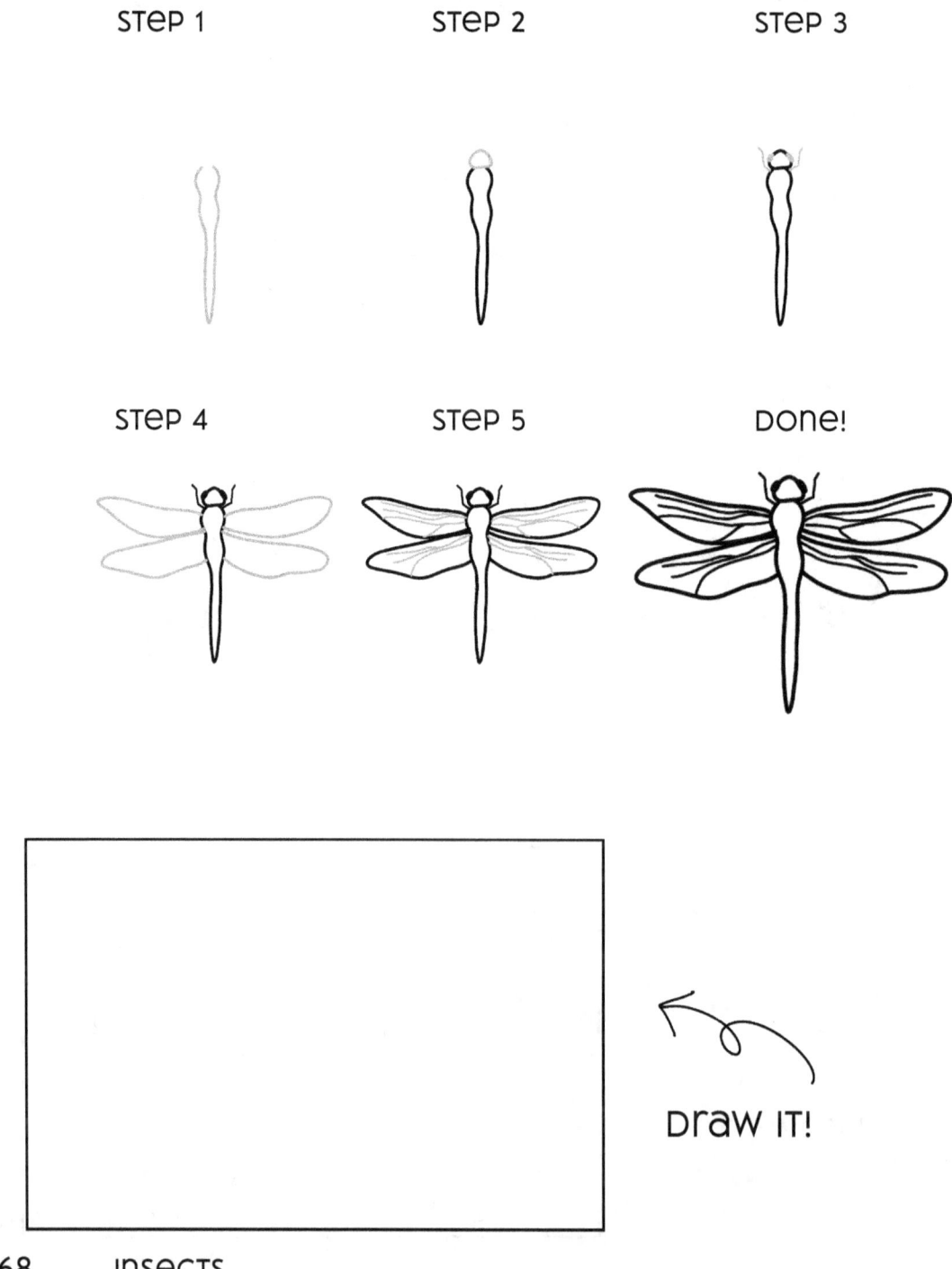

DRAW IT!

INSECTS

# DAMSELFLY

STEP 1

STEP 2

STEP 3

STEP 4

STEP 5

DONE!

DRAW IT!

# spider

STEP 1

STEP 2

STEP 3

STEP 4

STEP 5

Done!

Draw IT!

next up... prehistoric

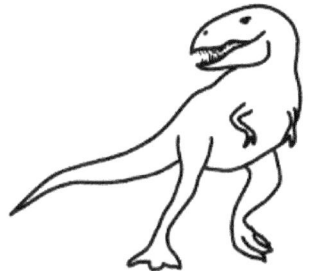

# PreHISTORIC

# TYrannosaurus rex

STEP 1          STEP 2          STEP 3

STEP 4          STEP 5          Done!

DRAW IT!

# PTERODACTYL

STEP 1

STEP 2

STEP 3

STEP 4

STEP 5

DONE!

DRAW IT!

# brontosaurus

STEP 1     STEP 2     STEP 3

STEP 4     STEP 5     Done!

Draw it!

# stegosaurus

STEP 1     STEP 2     STEP 3

STEP 4     STEP 5     done!

DRAW IT!

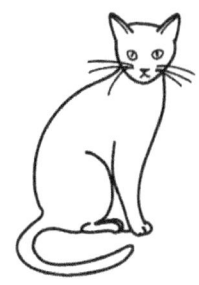 DOMESTIC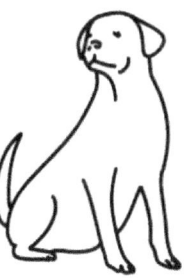

# DOMESTIC SHORT HAIR CAT

STEP 1

STEP 2

STEP 3

STEP 4

STEP 5

DONE!

DRAW IT!

# SPHYNX

STEP 1

STEP 2

STEP 3

STEP 4

STEP 5

DONE!

DRAW IT!

# SCOTTISH FOLD

STEP 1       STEP 2       STEP 3

STEP 4       STEP 5       Done!

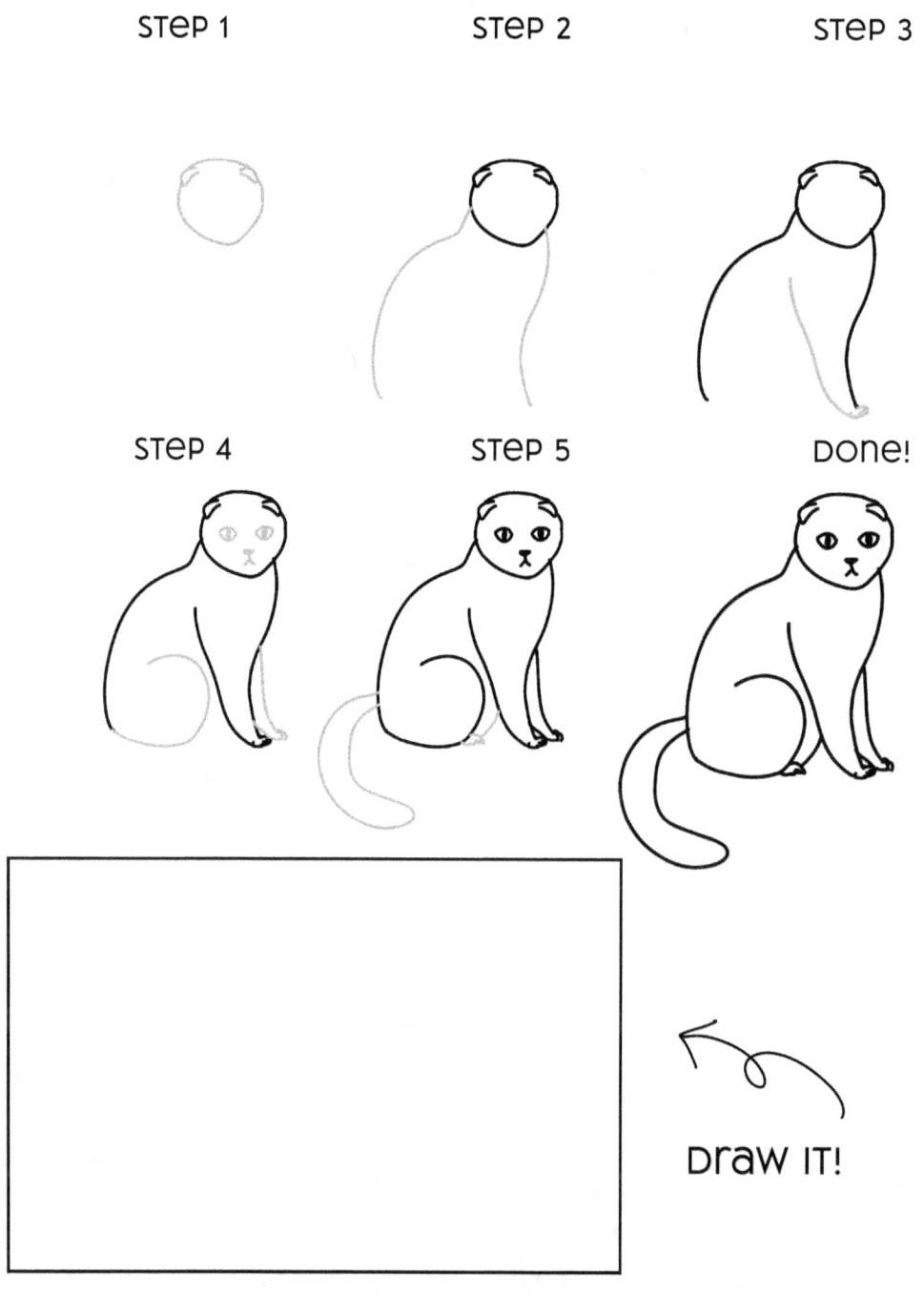

Draw it!

# persian

STEP 1  STEP 2  STEP 3

STEP 4  STEP 5  Done!

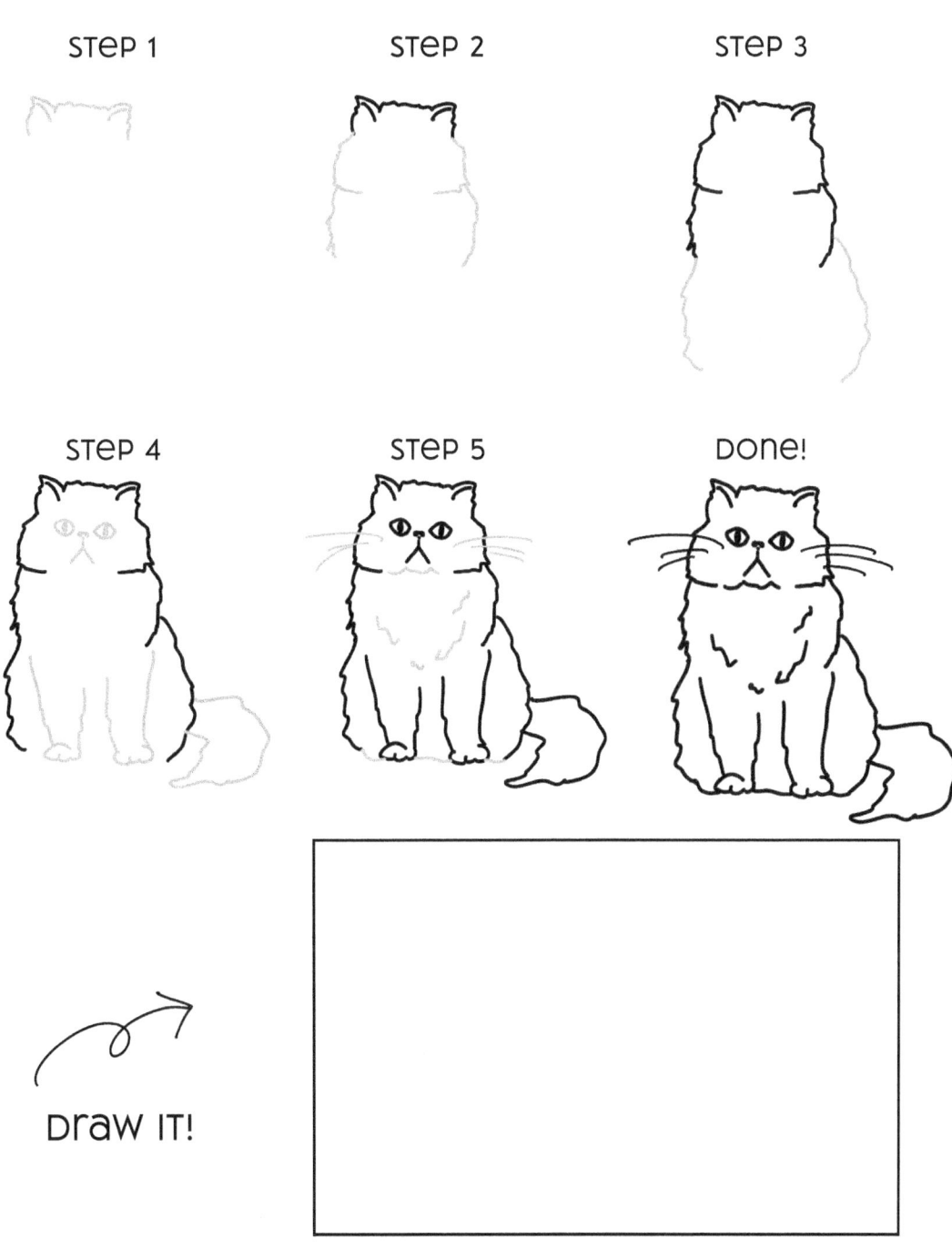

DRAW IT!

# BeaGLe

STEP 1

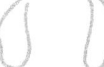

STEP 2

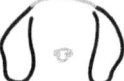

STEP 3

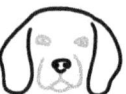

STEP 4

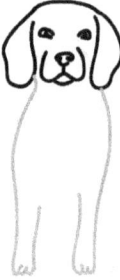

STEP 5

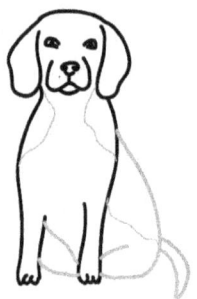

Done!

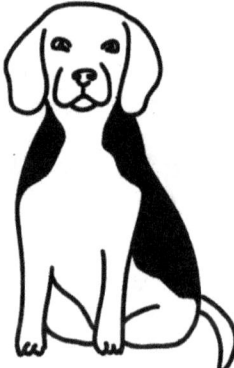

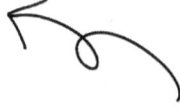

Draw IT!

DOMESTIC

# DaCHSHUND

STEP 1

STEP 2

STEP 3

STEP 4

STEP 5

Done!

Draw IT!

# PUG

STEP 1

STEP 2

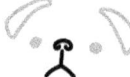

STEP 3

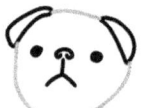

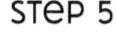

STEP 4

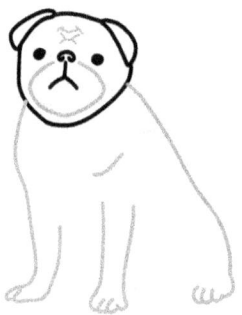

STEP 5

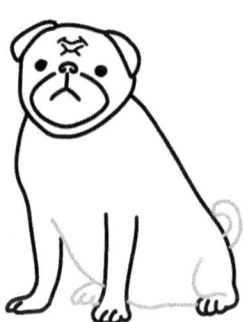

Done!

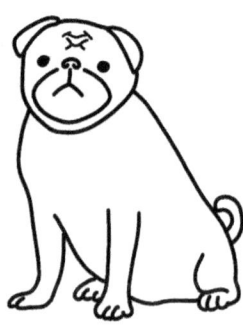

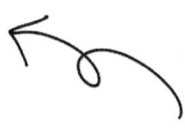

Draw it!

DOMESTIC

# German Shepherd

STEP 1    STEP 2    STEP 3

STEP 4    STEP 5    Done!

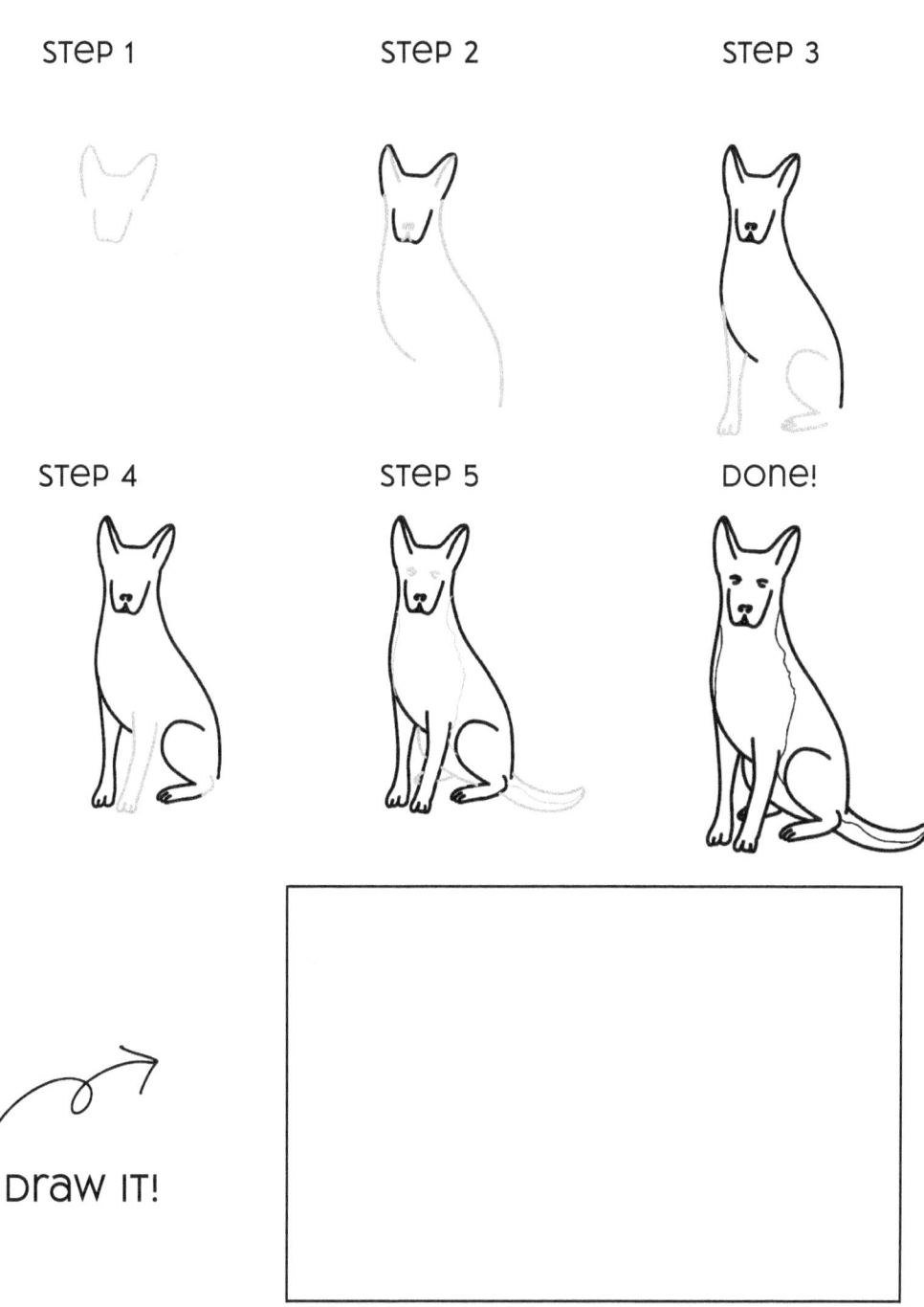

Draw it!

# Labrador

STEP 1

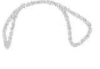

STEP 2

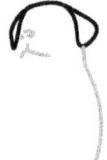

STEP 3

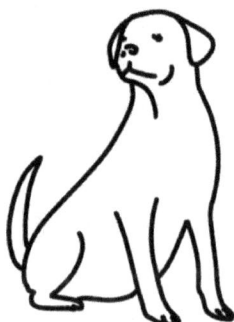

STEP 4

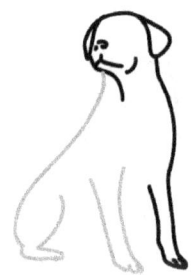

STEP 5

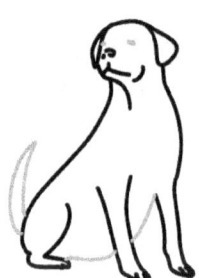

Done!

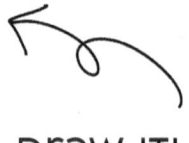

Draw it!

# CHIHUAHUA

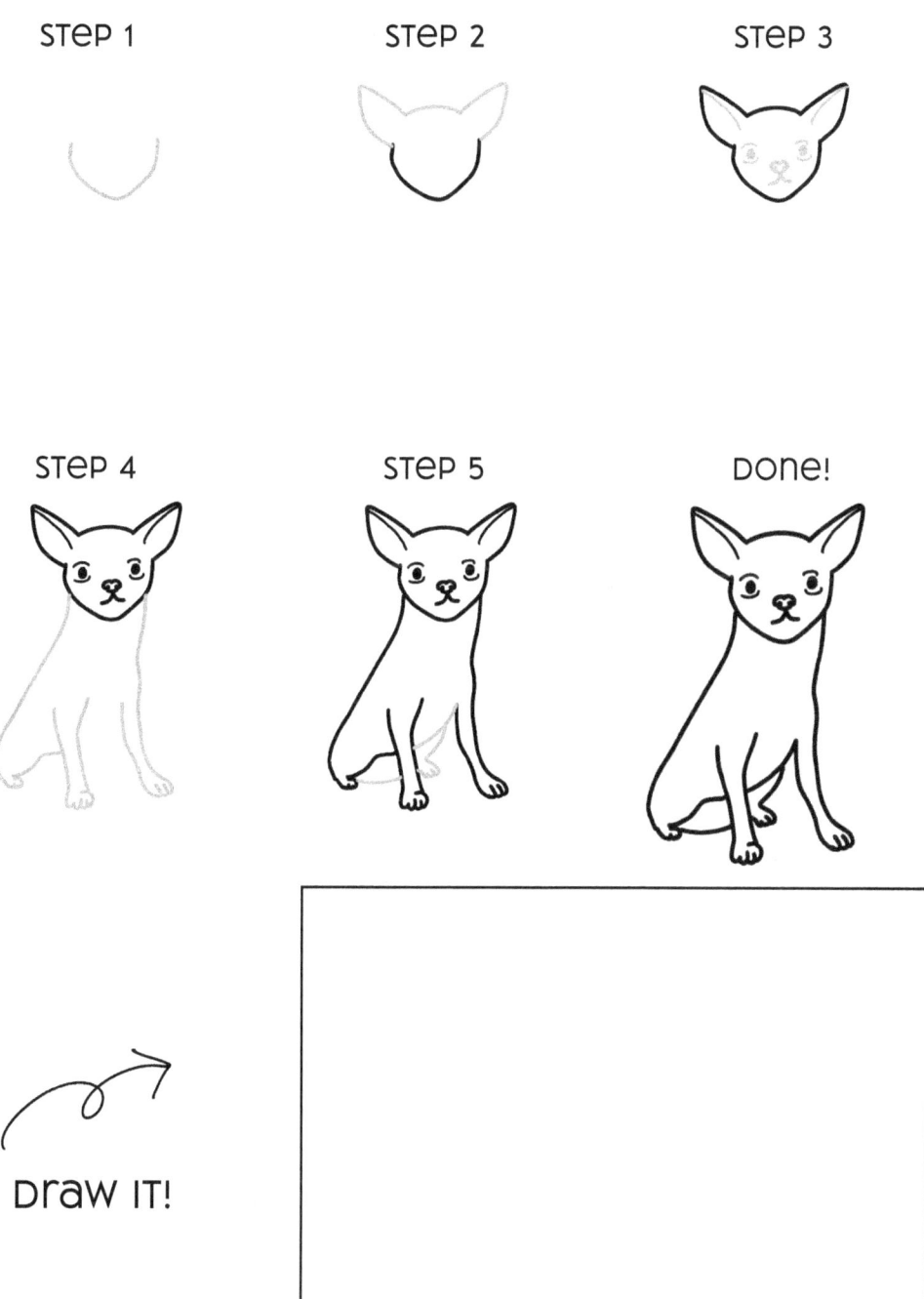

STEP 1

STEP 2

STEP 3

STEP 4

STEP 5

Done!

Draw IT!

# BOSTON TerrIer

STEP 1

STEP 2

STEP 3

STEP 4

STEP 5

DONE!

DRAW IT!

# COW

STEP 1

STEP 2

STEP 3

STEP 4

STEP 5

Done!

Draw It!

# PIG

STEP 1

STEP 2

STEP 3

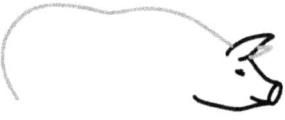

STEP 4

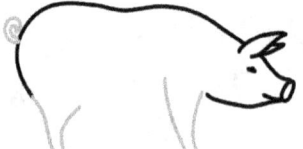

STEP 5

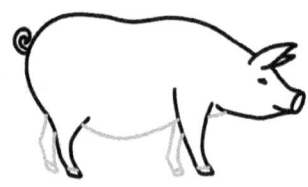

Done!

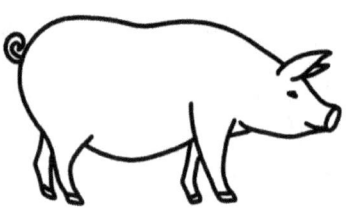

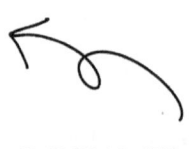

Draw it!

DOMESTIC

# HEY! I'M PEGGY.

I'm an artist, educator, and major animal lover. I am active in contributing to the rescue, rehabilitation and preservation of wildlife. I feel that it's incredibly important to speak up for those without a voice.

Learn lotttts more at www.thepigeonletters.com and follow me on instagram @thepigeonletters

see ya soon!

*Peggy Dean*

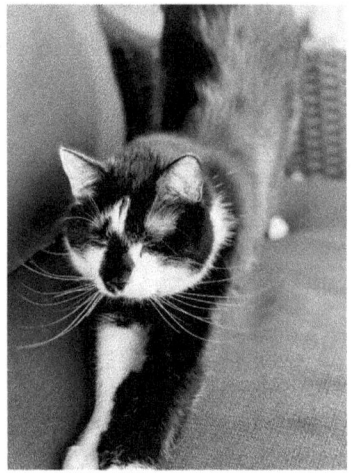

Here's LiTTLe eDie.
RememBeR, you DReW HeR FiRST. ;)

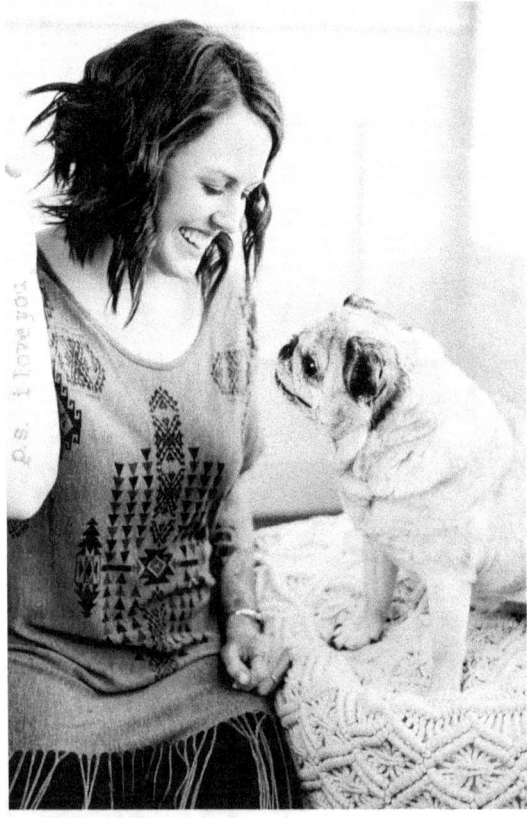

Here's my precious BaBy
angeL, Lucy THe Pug.

PHOTO BY Lauryn Kay PHOTOGraPHY

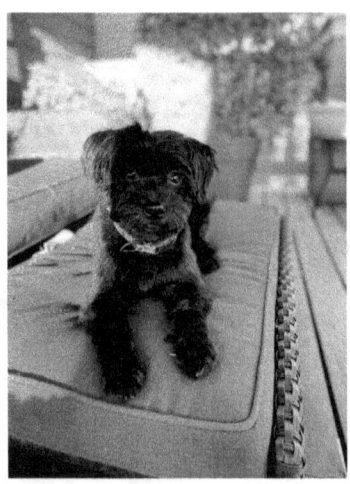

Here's BiLLie THe DOG.

# INDEX

www.ingramcontent.com/pod-product-compliance
Lightning Source LLC
Chambersburg PA
CBHW052033280526
45791CB00010B/2961